AT HOME IN STEEL

Residential Construction in Steel—Thoughts on Space and Structure

AT HOME IN STEEL

Residential Construction
in Steel—Thoughts
on Space and Structure

Zurich University of Applied Sciences /
Zürcher Hochschule für Angewandte
Wissenschaften
Institute of Constructive Design /
Institut Konstruktives Entwerfen (IKE)

With contributions by Ingrid Burgdorf,
Patric Fischli-Boson, Patric Furrer,
Stephan Mäder, Marcel Meili, Daniel
Meyer, Niko Nikolla, Tanja Reimer,
Astrid Staufer, and Martin Tschanz

PARK BOOKS

CONTENTS

p. 7 A "CRITICAL INVENTORY" OF STEEL IN RESIDENTIAL CONSTRUCTION
Foreword by Stephan Mäder

p. 9 STEEL IN RESIDENTIAL BUILDINGS: INTRODUCTION AND PROSPECTS
Daniel Meyer, Patric Fischli-Boson, Tanja Reimer, and Astrid Staufer in conversation

p. 21 ICONS OF STEEL CONSTRUCTION

p. 64 CONTEMPORARY STEEL BUILDINGS

A "Critical Inventory" of Steel in Residential Construction

The Institute of Constructive Design (IKE) of the Zurich University of Applied Sciences (ZHAW) has always been strongly interested in challenging and ostensibly less attractive issues in architecture, among them prefabrication in concrete, the pitched roof, the structure of thermal insulation, and the reuse of spolia and other materials. The decision to explore the application of steel in residential building in collaboration with the Swiss Center for Steel Construction (Stahlbau Zentrum Schweiz, SZS) is the result of the impartial curiosity and the commitment of the team of the Institute, under the direction of Astrid Staufer, to fathom unfamiliar phenomena in architecture. By a "critical inventory," we mean results of reading exemplary buildings so to speak backwards, re-creating the construction process from the end all the way back to the inception of planning, with the intention of making the new or rediscovered insights that come to light in the process public. The objects of this analysis are three icons of steel construction and nine contemporary steel buildings.

Concrete, masonry, wood, and steel are the classic construction materials for producing built structures, and are deployed in a variety of ways depending upon the region or building type. The joining and adding of tubular and planar elements and their cladding lead respectively—we contend—to different positions in architectural design. Given that the technical knowledge of steel construction is neglected in the training of architects and engineers, a reexamination of this topic in academic context seems well worthwhile. Pure steel construction, meanwhile, would amount to little more than a didactic finger exercise. The path toward discoveries that can be used in new approaches to building leads instead toward hybrid structures. A conscious and skillful application of steel should result in an expansion of the architectonic vocabulary, making it possible once again to break out of the monotony commonly encountered in architectural production.

For about ten years now, the mandate of technical universities and colleges has encompassed teaching, research as well as development, advanced training, and service provision. In the School of Architecture, Design and Civil Engineering, we aim for the reciprocal fertilization of research and development on the one hand with teaching on the other, and have at the same time taken up the mission of establishing international contacts. The first international summer workshop at IKE (in 2015) was an exemplary occasion in this regard, and one of great success, both internally and externally. The organizers invited long-standing friends and their students from renowned European architectural academies (Antwerp, Barcelona, Birmingham, and Guimarães) to come to Winterthur, where we assembled an excellent team consisting of representatives from teaching, practice, and research. The workshop facilitated playful but also serious approaches to our topic, its substantive findings are shown in the present publication—as an initial critical overview on the path toward further projects in teaching and research.

The organizers at the IKE deserve respect for their extraordinary commitment. They have strengthened contacts with our partner institutions, provided students with access to renowned architects and engineers, and in collaboration with the SZS made it possible for us to address new constructive and architectural themes.

Stephan Mäder, Dean, School of Architecture,
Design and Civil Engineering, 1998–2016

Steel in Residential Buildings: Introduction and Prospects

Tanja Reimer   Steel is rarely used in residential construction in Switzerland. What about this topic interested you as a group?

Astrid Staufer   We were asked by the Swiss Center for Steel Construction, the SZS, what we would wish for in the realm of steel buildings. What came to mind immediately were the "steel dreams" in modernist residential building—the Mies van der Rohe buildings, the Maison de Verre (p. 36), and the Eames House (p. 48)—and we expressed our regret over the fact that this field of design has been lost. Today, steel construction is only associated with commercial or industrial buildings.

Daniel Meyer   Steel fulfills many of today's construction demands in an optimal way. Requirements such as flexibility, separation of systems, short construction schedules, extended service life, and so forth, can be mastered superbly with steel construction.

Patric Fischli-Boson   And needless to say, the question posed by the SZS also has a commercial motivation, since steel contributes almost nothing to residential development at the moment. In of itself, however, that wouldn't be sufficient to launch such a project. As a civil engineer, I've often worked with steel, and enjoyed doing so. At some point, however, a certain boredom began to set in, a need to expand the range of possibilities.

Astrid Staufer   I can only support such a desire for diversification: at the Institute, of course, we're not concerned exclusively with steel construction. In the search for specificity of expression, we would simply like to have a maximally broad palette in our hands. With regard to residential development, steel is essentially absent today. With the Solothurn School, we witnessed the final impulse towards steel building in Switzerland, after which it slipped away from us—and today, the material is primarily associated with the theme of dematerialization, with anonymous glass-and-steel complexes. We are interested in precisely the opposite: the presence of the material, and how it can be exploited for the sake of architectural expressiveness.

Patric Fischli-Boson   The Solothurn School may have achieved a great deal for steel construction, but in one respect its members blocked their own further development. The modular systems, which predetermined a great deal, are still stuck in the minds of architects, and work as a deterrent. Contemporary production engineering in digital building allows precisely the reverse: all desired forms and connections become possible, without being reflected in building costs.

Astrid Staufer   After concluding our research, I was actually astonished by the diverse ways in which steel has already been used. Whether the planar application of the material by Martin Bühler (p. 106) or its systemic revitalization by Jürg Graser (p. 136)—this "search along the margins" has shown that enormous potential lies dormant here.

THE CONDITIONS FOR A CULTURE
OF STEEL CONSTRUCTION

Tanja Reimer   Why do we build so little with steel—compared to England, for example? Martin Mensinger and Chris Snow have argued that there, they don't know how to build with concrete,[1] and here, we don't know how to build with steel. What is your view?

Patric Fischli-Boson   In terms of tendency, I would agree. Also, steel construction involves higher initial expenses than solid construction, which puts people off.

Astrid Staufer   In recent decades, an impressive academic building tradition has formed in Switzerland. But it may be precisely the tectonic demand to avoid cladding constructions that has led toward field research on steel as a material being shortchanged.

Tanja Reimer   At the same time, Chris Snow and Jürg Graser have imputed a certain laziness to architects when it comes to grappling with issues of construction, which then promotes solid construction. Does that seem plausible to you?

Astrid Staufer   I don't believe the cause has been laziness. In recent years, a rampant mania for standardization and certification has however meant that architects have been absorbed by other questions to such a degree that a passion for constructive issues seems to have been neglected somewhat as a result. We will need to recapture this concern. If we want to avoid being restricted to designing stage sets that are positioned in front of bricolage structures!

Patric Fischli-Boson   I do perceive one tendency that could promote steel construction: digital building and BIM share a similar intensity curve and high initial investments with steel construction. Already during training, moreover, prejudice must be converted into curiosity.

Astrid Staufer   The promotion of steel construction in teaching is very important, but even more useful are attractive practical examples. As soon as these emerge, both students and architects will become interested in steel construction again.

COST-EFFECTIVE BUILDING IN STEEL

Tanja Reimer   We encountered exemplary contemporary instances, primarily in the high-priced market segment. Is it also possible to build affordable housing in steel?

Patric Fischli-Boson   In fact, we have found very few cost-effective residential buildings in Switzerland. On the other hand, I know of highly cost-effective examples in Luxembourg and France, and I see no reason why such experiences from abroad can't be adapted here.

Tanja Reimer   How do they build cost-effectively there?

Patric Fischli-Boson   As a rule, it's a question of continuous supports with prefabricated ceiling systems. The result is a simple support-panel system that, as a skeleton, generates enormous freedom.

Daniel Meyer I believe steel construction is per se just as economical as masonry or concrete. It simply requires, as the primary structure, secondary elements that must be combined skillfully with one another in order to satisfy acoustic and thermal demands, as well as fire-protection regulations. It fails as soon as we fail to build in a genuinely hybrid fashion.

Astrid Staufer But isn't it then necessary to economize elsewhere, since steel construction calls for cladding? Isn't steel economical only with very large spans?

Patric Fischli-Boson When we think of steel-concrete composite construction, we actually need spans of around 11 meters before it pays off, but with other adequate solutions, such as prefabricated ceiling elements, which also incorporate acoustic elements, we can definitely build economically with smaller spans—from 6 to 7 meters.

Tanja Reimer The example of Lacaton & Vassal (p. 76) features such a concept, but achieves a far lower structural standard than is customary in Switzerland. Should we call our standards into question while nonetheless fulfilling our responsibilities toward residents?

Astrid Staufer Absolutely. The technologized building, which transforms us into passive inhabitants, does not contribute to a sustainable future. We must heighten awareness again of what comfort actually means. And take the reins into our own hands rather than surrendering blindly to multiplying norms and labels.

Daniel Meyer We need standards, but it's important that they be understood simply as boundaries within which one can move in order to open up new maneuverability.

INTELLIGENTLY COMPOSED HYBRIDS

Tanja Reimer   You mentioned above that the potential and the challenges lie in a hybrid manner of building. How can thermal comfort be improved in a steel building?

Daniel Meyer   I explicitly oppose terms such as "barracks climate"—which, for me, have nothing to do with steel or lightweight construction. The materials must be deployed where they are strong. Steel can be used in conjunction with concrete, when mass is required—this is well known. A combination of steel, wood, and concrete is also interesting. Here, steel girders work together with wood-concrete compound ceilings. This makes it possible to control many factors in a highly efficient way: fire protection, comfort, and acoustics.

Tanja Reimer   In multistory apartment buildings, fire protection seems to be a big challenge. Which concepts look promising for the future?

Patric Fischli-Boson   The more I deal with this issue, the more I feel that the common view—that it's complicated—is primarily motivated by the fact that fire safety is resolved without any effort when building with concrete. With steel construction, you have to know more, but the fire load can be reduced, for example, via natural fire modeling,[2] and fire resistance can be achieved through concrete encasement, secondary structures, or membrane action. Beyond coatings, many concepts are particularly well-suited to residential development.

Daniel Meyer   I see enormous architectural potential with concrete encasement in particular. I would be interested in learning how it could be used for architectural expression apart from industrial building. The steel remains present, and one could work with shadow joints or dye the concrete.

Astrid Staufer   That's a good point! To search for the beauty of hybrid structures in the intelligence of their joining principles seems to be a totally unexploited field.

Tanja Reimer   Last semester, we had students who worked on the spatial impact of various fire-safety solutions—from chamber concrete to a combination of cladding and coatings, inspired by the Maison de Verre. Because they were unable to escape into the design of apartments, they had to engage in this confrontation, and ultimately developed a design approach for it. In a certain sense, this reinforces the suspicion that constructive research is often overpowered by other topics …

Astrid Staufer   The development of intelligently composed hybrids requires enormously hard work and ingenious, detailed knowledge, so that the relevant material properties are optimally effective, and the result is also beautiful.

Daniel Meyer   That holds true for engineers as well as for architects.

CONSTRUCTIVE RESEARCH IN DESIGN

Tanja Reimer   With the icons, we were impressed by the constructive research that takes place in design, propelled by new conditions of production. In the Hôtel Tassel (p. 22), Horta combined cast iron and rolled sections in a single construction element. The Eames exploited new developments from the war years for residential construction. Where do we find new possibilities today?

Astrid Staufer   It's a question of exhausting the specific limits of the material through the concrete conditions of the project. Steel construction as a catalog of standard profiles can no longer be the future. But perhaps computer-aided production can really assist us in this investigation, yet without us having to surrender our responsibility.

Patric Fischli-Boson   We discovered, for example, that it can be more economical to have segments of sheet metal welded by robots rather than using standard profiles. In fact, you are no longer tied to the catalog, but are instead relatively free.

Daniel Meyer   What is nonetheless no longer possible from an economic perspective is the omnidirectional cross pillars of Mies in flat rolled steel, with their spatial qualities. As soon as the flanges are omitted, they become uneconomical, because the mass of the profiles is incorrectly dispersed. To develop convincing and efficient sections with architects is a very exciting task.

Patric Fischli-Boson   On the other hand, I still find it interesting to use and configure existing manufactured products in new ways. In this respect, the Eames House is still highly topical, and I'm also fascinated by the corner constructions using standard profiles in the buildings of Mies.

Astrid Staufer   That's an important addendum. Such a "creative bricolage" certainly shows great potential in the context of low-cost residential building, in that it identifies elements which are capable of supplementing existing catalog products and deploying them in optimal ways. At the same time, the reshaping of standard profiles means a kind of balancing act. We discussed intensively whether the sheet metal welded over the sharp-edged H-profile, as Made in architects applied it (p. 146), is still materially appropriate. One could, however, argue that this results in a specifically "metallic" expression. The discussion about which measures are appropriate to which purpose, and which are not, must be conducted continuously.

Daniel Meyer   Another aspect is joining. The joining principles of the existing profiles have been more or less exhausted—you can weld them or screw them together. Particularly in machine engineering, nonetheless, there are interesting connections, for example, the blind hole threads, which—in conjunction with the corresponding milled holes and full steel elements— produce perfect, almost seamless joints.

Tanja Reimer   … in the sense of an abstraction.

Astrid Staufer   But wouldn't the reverse be more interesting? With other ways of building, the joints are suppressed. The "steel-specific" could mean to satisfy the revived yearning for ornamentation through the visualization of these connections. Chareau consistently staged connections between steel elements, deliberately calling attention to them.

Daniel Meyer   Earlier, this was taken so far that riveted girders were supplemented with pop rivets as ornamentation. Moreover, steel back then was always cast—this was turned to account back then for entire nodes. Joints can also be highlighted visually through the alternation of surfaces such as cast or rolled material.

INTERIOR TECTONICS AND COMFORT

Tanja Reimer What can tectonics contribute to comfort?

Astrid Staufer When it comes to questions of comfort and coziness, steel construction can't resolve this alone. It would be nice to be able once again to explicitly thematize the relationship between loadbearing and cladding and hence to achieve a contemporary elegance that could be a desirable motif in residential building in contrast to solidity.

Patric Fischli-Boson But is elegance the right word? Using steel construction tectonically, a student group achieved an industrial, outré atmosphere that surely displayed a certain charm.

Tanja Reimer Perhaps it is precisely this polarity between savagery and delicacy that needs to be investigated?

Astrid Staufer Yes, it's this aspect of delicacy that can assume a variety of forms.

Daniel Meyer In teaching, I also observe a search for more tectonics in interior spaces. It's interesting what happens here: you still design in concrete, and replace the thin, flat ceiling slab with a ribbed slab, but without expanding the spans correspondingly. The result is a relatively solid concrete ceiling. If this is a new tendency, then steel construction certainly offers some competition while being more elegant.

Astrid Staufer In my view, this yearning for tectonics is related to a desire to carry over multiple demands into a kind of organizational system. A subdivided ceiling seems desirable in order to single out areas that can be devoted to acoustics, illumination, etc. Steel could prove useful in shaping a complex whole in a way that is more optically manifest.

INTERDISCIPLINARITY

Tanja Reimer It appears that steel construction can only be developed further through collaboration involving various disciplines. How do things stand with regard to interdisciplinarity?

Daniel Meyer In my view, the biggest problem is that today, engineers no longer can elaborate steel construction on their own, nor do they want to. Already during the project phase, they send sketches on planning and detailing to the contractor. For me, this is an inconceivable practice. Like architects, I regard myself as a generalist who develops the concept and the details and implements them in collaboration with the contractor.

Patric Fischli-Boson   I can endorse that. When did this unfavorable development begin?

Daniel Meyer   I assume it is also related to remuneration. For a concrete ceiling, as a rule, you have to prepare three supporting documents. With steel construction and hybrid constructions in general, there are also all of the connections, the stability, buckling, canting, bending, and torsional flexural bending—it is enormously laborious. It is avoided because commensurate fees are not available, or because one has made an offer that is too low.

Astrid Staufer   On the side of the architect, it's of course the case that steel and hybrid methods of construction in general only have a chance when we conduct a dialogue with the engineer from the very beginning. The conditions must fertilize the design. Which is why an acceptance of responsibility in each discipline is essential—and a designing hand that holds everything together.

Daniel Meyer   Good interdisciplinarity functions only when each participant has a reliable grasp of his own discipline and is familiar with the rules of collaboration.

Tanja Reimer   And what about the contractor?

Daniel Meyer   That's important as well, of course. With complex building projects, you have to involve him early on—but in order to pose questions, not to request planning services.

Tanja Reimer   In the end, it's clear that more curiosity and boldness will be required on all sides if steel is to make progress in residential building as well.

Astrid Staufer   Incidentally, that's not just true for steel construction. All modular building methods have a hard time, because at an early point in time they demand more intellectual effort from us, the planners. Prefabricated concrete construction also requires enormous powers of persuasion from our side in relation to other participating planners.

Daniel Meyer That's because it's a question of joining, not casting. You have to develop nodes, which can be enormously exciting, but requires a great deal of hard work.

Astrid Staufer The art of joining[3]—yes, we'd better start to get some practice again!

1 Chris Snow was the project architect with Jonathan Woolf Architects for the Brick Leaf House (p. 96), and Martin Mensinger is a professor for steel construction at the TU Munich. Both were guests and discussion partners at the summer workshop organized by the ZHAW in 2015.
2 In contrast to the ISO fire temperature curve, the natural fire model takes into account the essential factors that influence the progression of a natural fire, such as the type and number of fire loads, the geometry of the fire space, the thermal features of the surrounding structural elements, etc. With the help of this model, it becomes possible to carry out a far more realistic technical fire-protection calculation of the supporting structure.
3 "Die Kunst des Fügens", in the original German text, is a play on words of Bach's late musical work *The Art of the Fugue.*

ICONS OF STEEL CONSTRUCTION

1 HÔTEL TASSEL BY VICTOR HORTA 1893–1896, BRUSSELS

Martin Tschanz   p. 22

2 MAISON DE VERRE BY PIERRE CHAREAU 1928–1932, PARIS

Ingrid Burgdorf   p. 36

3 EAMES HOUSE BY CHARLES & RAY EAMES 1949, LOS ANGELES

Marcel Meili   p. 48

1

HÔTEL TASSEL   VICTOR HORTA   22

HÔTEL TASSEL　　　VICTOR HORTA

HÔTEL TASSEL   VICTOR HORTA   26

Iron in a Not Entirely Bourgeois Residence

Victor Horta's Hôtel Tassel figures in virtually every history of modern architecture, and is acknowledged as one of the most stylistically formative works of Art Nouveau. For the most part, the focus of attention is on the house's ornamental forms. And although most historians would not go as far as Nikolaus Pevsner, who regarded Horta as "if not wholly, at least primarily, a decorator,"[1] then the house does seem, from that perspective, to serve principally to illustrate a short-lived and ultimately superficial trend. It is also seen, however, as a precursor of the modernist architecture of the 20th century. And subsequently, it was judged in relation to these principles. Sigfried Giedion, for example, recognized its flexible layout and perceived in this openness—made possible by its iron structure—a forerunner of the Corbusian *plan libre*.[2] The analytical separation of structure and spatial formation that is so characteristic of the *plan libre* is, however, wholly alien to the architecture of Horta. It aims not toward the division and clarification of the elements, but instead toward a synthesis within which the support structure, the ornamentation, the color scheme, the surfaces, not least of all the illumination are elevated into a spatio-artistic whole, one that responds with precision in both plan and section to a specific program (p. 30). If anything, this arrangement is comparable with Adolf Loos's *Raumplan* rather than the open floor plan.[3] The Hôtel Tassel is full of complexity and contradiction, and precisely by virtue of a lack of consistency when it comes to serving the whole, the building is of particular interest today.[4]

1   Nikolaus Pevsner, *Pioneers of Modern Design: From William Morris to Walter Gropius* (Harmondsworth: Penguin Books, 1960), 1st ed. 1936, p. 98.
2   Sigfried Giedion, *Space, Time, and Architecture: The Growth of a New Tradition* (Cambridge: Harvard University Press, 1941), pp. 298–302, esp. p. 301.
3   This was perceived already by Robert Delevoy, who nonetheless also characterized the *Raumplan* as a forerunner of the open floor plan. Robert L. Delevoy, *Victor Horta* (Brussels: Elsevier, 1958), p. 8.
4   Concerning the inadequate reception of his achievement, Horta is not entirely free of guilt. The Hôtel Tassel—despite being relatively well documented—was published without section views and often with incomplete layouts. Missing in Wasmuth's *Neubauten in Brüssel* (Berlin: Wasmuth, 1900), pl. 14, for example, is the mezzanine level—and subsequently, from Giedion and others as well. The situation was not improved when, in 1945, Horta disposed of his personal archive as wastepaper—especially since most of his works have been destroyed or are only accessible today to an extremely restricted degree.

A SPECTACLE OF TECTONICS AND STAGED MOVEMENT

It is not easy to describe a complex whole. Let us begin with the iron columns at the heart of the house, which are not accidentally its best-known and most frequently illustrated elements. They simultaneously embody the new elegant formal idiom, as well as the innovation of using exposed iron elements in domestic construction. The visitor encounters them upon entering the house along its central axis, passing through a small porch and arriving in an octagonal vestibule past a laterally situated cloakroom. Opening itself up to him here, as he faces the light, is a view into the depths of the house (p. 23). At this point, seven steps rise to the level of the salon and dining room; the ascent is framed on both sides by elegantly curved iron girders. Below, the space opens toward the sides onto the conservatory on one hand and onto the stair hall on the other (pp. 24-25).

It is here that the above-mentioned iron columns stand. As fully sculptural elements, they bundle together the longitudinal and transverse orientations of the space, both articulated by iron girders, inviting the visitor to circumnavigate them. Given the oval plan of the columns, the transverse direction is particularly active. The profile, although cast in a single piece, seems so to speak composite or pulled apart,[5] which relieves the cruciform supports of the girders above the capitals. We see a tectonic structure in which the curving rolled sections interpenetrate organically, allowing them to be simply riveted together. Articulated here is the convergence and synergy between the girders, even though the loads are entirely or primarily taken by the cast-iron core of the construction, which remains for the most part concealed.

This theater of tectonics is spatially active. The iron elements clearly appear as the supporting structure, but just as much as guides to a sense of movement by bundling and giving direction to the spatial tensions. Only incidentally do the columns seem to support the lattice girders, themselves just barely reminiscent of classical beams. Its asymmetrical arc accompanies the upward movement, which is counteracted by a complex, vaulted ceiling that links the mezzanine with the central space. Below, the curve of the beam begins with an expressively shaped support, while above, it does not fully terminate with the support, but flows instead into a U-profile, which frames the wall, with curved elements in between. As a result, the movement is continued and brought all the way down to the floor, while the visitor encounters the face sides of the U-profiles frontally, which brakes his forward momentum into the house.

The light that streams in from above on both sides allows the middle area, framed by the columns and their beams, to appear as a kind of inserted pavilion that is open toward the sides. The mirror on the front side of the conservatory doubles the space along the transverse axis of the house, generating an interplay between the real and painted plants, the iron palms of the col-

---

5   This theme is varied on the façade, where the iron "colonnettes" of the bow window are in fact
     assembled from individual profiles.

HÔTEL TASSEL   VICTOR HORTA   28

umns and the ascending tendril ornamentation of the stair hall. The motif of organic growth is omnipresent. It activates the vertical, and is reinforced by the color scheme of the wall, inviting us to ascend.

But the spectacle of tectonics, sketched above, tells only half the story. The iron structure comprises not only those elements that are identified chromatically as loadbearing elements and frames for openings, but also the surfaces in between, which appear as filling. The plan reveals that the supports of the iron loadbearing structure consist—apart from the two columns—of intricately shaped hollow elements. In essence rhombic, they appear to have been assembled from U-profiles and connecting sheet metal elements (p. 32). Sculpturally elaborated ornamental details in the dining room, however, suggest that the designation "cast iron" (*fonte*) in the pre-construction drawings is to be taken literally, and that despite the complex form, the supports consist of single cast elements.[6] Beyond this, the hot air heating is integrated into it as well, with air vents in the planar parts that are articulated as wall elements. While Horta was clearly oriented toward Viollet-le-Duc's *Entretiens sur l'architecture* in shaping his iron structure,[7] it is also apparent that he was interested in Viollet-le-Duc's rationalism only to the degree that it accommodated his spatial intentions. He overlaid the tectonic system with a spatial intention, and without allowing either one to become dominant.

PROGRAM AND SPACE FORMATION

With the Hôtel Tassel, Horta's task was to "build a bourgeois residence for a bachelor." The latter lived with his grandmother, and received a lively circle of friends that was restricted to preferred scientists and artists.[8] Tassel, a professor of descriptive geometry and a leading mathematician and physicist of his time, belonged to a circle of progressive scientists which the chemist and entrepreneur Ernest Solvay had gathered around himself. A particularly intimate friendship developed between Tassel and Charles Lefébure, Solvay's private secretary, who was a great alpinist and a passionate photographer. Lefébure seems to have inspired the building and contributed to its spatial program; in Horta's memoirs, he is mentioned almost as a second client.[9]

6   During the brief visit to the house that was granted to us, moreover under strict supervision, this question could not be ultimately clarified. Without a detailed investigation, any unambiguous identification of wrought iron, rolled sections (to some extent additionally forged) and cast elements is impossible. On Horta's iron structures, see also Quentin Collette et al., "Victor Horta's Iron Architecture: A Structural Analysis," in: *Advanced Materials Research,* vol. 133/134 (2010), pp. 373–378.

7   Eugène Emmanuel Viollet-le-Duc, *Entretiens sur l'architecture* (Paris: Morel, 1863–1872). At the university, Horta succeeded a student of Viollet-le-Duc, and his instruction was based in essential ways on the latter's theories.

8   Victor Horta, *Mémoires: Texte établi, annoté et introduit par Cécile Duilière* (Brussels: Ministère de la Communauté Française de Belgique, Administration du Patrimoine Culturel, 1985), p. 34: "[…] construire une maison bourgeoise pour un célibataire qui, tout en vivant avec sa grand-mère, reçoit ses amis avec joie en un cercle fermé qui ne s'ouvre que pour s'élargir à des savants ou des artistes dont la présence ajoute à l'intérêt déjà acquis des réunions." Research into the city registry however suggests that the grandmother recalled by Horta was actually an aunt. Cf. Michèle Goslar, *Victor Horta 1861–1947: l'homme, l'architecte, l'art nouveau* (Brussels: Fondation Pierre Lahaut, 2012), p. 91, n. 243. Horta composed his memoirs only very late in life.

9   Horta, *Mémoires* (see n. 8), p. 34.

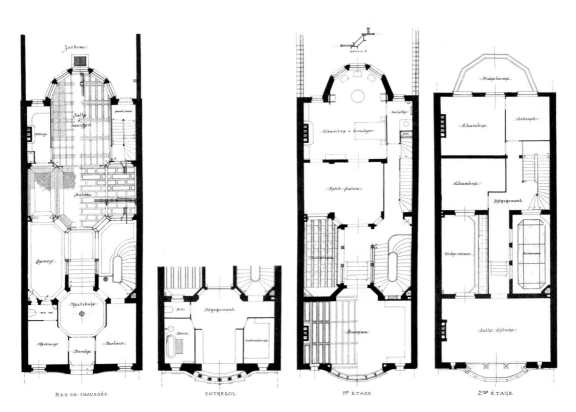
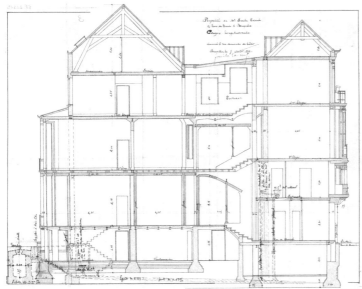

Above: layout of ground floor, mezzanine level, and 1st and 2nd upper stories; below: section

HÔTEL TASSEL   VICTOR HORTA   30

The circle around Tassel was regarded as emphatically freethinking, with almost anarchistic traits.[10] The client by no means corresponded to conventional notions of bourgeois values. This may have been the deeper reason for the house's radically introverted character, whose scandal was less a question of the symmetry of the façade, the bow window, or the visible use of iron—although all of these elements were novel in the context of the typology of Brussels townhouses. The truly extraordinary feature was the absence of any visible *piano nobile*. The large window in the second upper story belongs to a workroom, while in place of the living area that should have faced the street in representative fashion was a low mezzanine, whose stained-glass windows shrouded the life taking place within in mystery (p. 22). Situated here is a smoking salon, modeled on a Turkish *sedir* (upholstered bench), its back turned demonstratively toward the street, while within, deep views onto the living and salon areas open up from an intimate niche. This space, which lies along the central axis of the house, is flanked by a bathroom and a darkroom, and at times the shaft of light from a projector supplanted the line of sight of the smokers. It cast an image from the gallery[11] through the smoking salon and the open door of the dining room, where a canvas could be mounted in such instances, converting it into a stage with a framing backdrop.[12]

With justice, Alphonse Balat—Horta's revered master—compared the house's façade to a pregnant woman. It seems to bulge outward under internal pressure.[13] The iron elements are embedded into the stone front that faces the street, constituting little more than a discreet hint at the iron structure. Despite the large windows, the inner life of this "expectant" house remains concealed from view. For those who do not know the house, it remains opaque—although the façade is its faithful reflection.[14]

Revealed in a section view is a complex that is more reminiscent of the typology of the Zähringen towns than of the typical Brussels townhouses, with its arrangement of three laterally accessible rooms, one set behind the next. There is a front house containing workrooms, and a rear building containing living and bedrooms (p. 30). We can speak of a separating courtyard, however, only with reference to the upper stories, which are carefully concealed from the more public spaces. Below, to be sure, the house is also illuminated from its central zone, which is, however, fully integrated into the representative sequence of spaces. The longitudinal and transverse axes of the house intersect in the room that is flanked by iron columns, where our viewing of the house had its starting point. The English term "landing" is

10 David Albert Hanser, *The Early Works of Victor Horta: The Origins of Art Nouveau Architecture*, PhD Diss. (Urbana, 1994), pp. 183–193, here p. 187, relying upon a manuscript by Henry van de Velde, who was a friend of Lefébure's.
11 A section of the balustrade latticework can be folded back in order to facilitate the projection.
12 It is not entirely clear whether the projections were viewed from the salon, or as rear projections from the dining room: "[…] conférences illustrées par clichés photographiques, projetés au fond du salon et de la salle à manger où l'audience prenait place." Horta, *Mémoires* (see n. 8), p. 38.
13 Goslar, *Victor Horta 1861–1947* (see n. 8), p. 106; Hanser, *The Early Works of Victor Horta* (see n. 10), p. 202.
14 Cf. Horta, *Mémoires* (see n. 8), pp. 37–39.

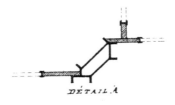

Above left: room sequence of dining room, salon, conservatory; above right: detail of the iron supports between salon and dining room; below: detailed view of the ceilings of the salon (left) and dining room (right).

HÔTEL TASSEL   VICTOR HORTA   32

apposite: in fact, one arrives under an elegant baldachin, and moreover in the middle of the house. And almost finds oneself, however, in an external space!

IRON AND ATMOSPHERE

Horta plays up this ambivalence. For his Royal Greenhouses, Horta's teacher Alphonse Balat integrated classic stone columns, a festival hall, a dining room, and even a church into his enormous iron and glass complex.[15] Horta now integrated iron, glass, and a garden into a stone townhouse. Here, iron is not simply an efficient resource for maintaining structural slenderness and coming to terms economically with the narrow parcel. It is also a rhetorical resource, which is exploited in order to create atmospheric spaces. In the conservatory, the above-described spectacle of tectonics is enacted in such a way that the space's theme is its lightweight, well-lit structure. It is not least the iron, painted green and adorned with gold, which makes a "greenhouse" of the roofed courtyard.[16] But the separation between the conservatory and the salon already has an ambivalent character. It is readable as an open framework, but just as much as a folded wall, not unlike a folding screen. The glass panes set in frames are to be sure transparent, but also reflective, and are supplemented on the salon side by curtains. One section of the openings, moreover, is configured as a display case (p. 26).[17]

From the perspective of the salon, the glass wall has a different character than the view from the conservatory. Here, as well, to be sure, individual elements of the structure are displayed as a framework; others, however, are situated as a wall, and in such a way that the pink of the framework and the floral decorative painting of the wall surfaces are coordinated with one another chromatically. The result is an ambiguity that is at its strongest where the structure develops its greatest depth. Here, the theme of tectonics is deprived of its significance, while the theme of spatial delimitation becomes more important (p. 32).

In the dining room, finally, the articulation of—or rather, allusion to—the iron structure is restricted to the contoured edges, which flow into sculpturally-formed, capital-style leaf motifs. Otherwise, the ironwork disappears behind wallpaper or behind colored surfaces that are adapted to it: the theme of the space-containing wall becomes dominant. The pattern and greenish color of the wallpaper[18] create a link with the conservatory, but here the vegetal motif is an element of a surface ornamentation—flowers, not stalks—and hence corresponds entirely to the convention of a bourgeois

---

15   Cf. Edgar Goedleven, *Die Königlichen Gewächshäuser von Laeken-Brüssel* (Eupen: Grenz-Echo, 1989).

16   In the drawings for the building permit, Horta still calls the conservatory a "cour couverte" ("covered courtyard") and in the publication plan a "serre" ("greenhouse").

17   The first pictures show a gracile, open framework; a later photograph shows glass shelves and a small heating element.

18   David Hanser has identified the pattern as Charles Voysey's "Elaine." See Hanser, *The Early Works of Victor Horta* (see n. 10), p. 282. It was Henry van de Velde who procured the wallpaper, manufactured by Morris. During the restoration of 1983–1985, it was replaced by coloristically similar but more tranquil Morris wallpapers. See François Loyer, Jean Delhaye, *Victor Horta: Hôtel Tassel 1893–1895* (Brussels: Aux Archives d'Architecture Moderne, 1986), pp. 35, 97.

living room. Also adapted to it is the wooden beam ceiling, whose iron edge profiles are masked by imitative painting (p. 32).

In the Hôtel Tassel, Horta seems to have systematically investigated the potential expressive forms of iron in domestic construction, from the explicit if not full exposure of the structure in the conservatory all the way to its near total masking in the dining room. The salon, with its glass walls on the one side and doors on the other, assumes an intermediate position, with regard to character as well. It hardly surprises that its design was, patently, no easy matter for Horta. In his memoirs, he mentions a failed attempt at a relief "à l'égyptienne."[19] Subsequently, he evidently attempted with the iris motif to create a link with the theme of the painting in the stair hall and conservatory, albeit in a more delicate and tranquil variation.[20] A further attempt, also known only in fragmentary form, displays figural painting: a Bacchic scene and a procession led by a triton; it too was ultimately abandoned.[21] The solution that was finally chosen combines the wallpaper used in the dining room with a planar, relatively severe decorative painting featuring flower motifs, achieving a certain ease in mediating between the conservatory and the room.

TRANSPARENCY AND AMBIVALENCE

The representative rooms in the Hôtel Tassel are characterized by transparency. Thanks to the diaphanous quality of the lightweight construction and the glass walls, the entire depth of the house can be grasped at a glance, and the salon extends all the way to the point at which the ceiling of the mezzanine level forms a kind of artificial horizon. More important than transparency in the literal sense, however, are those spatial superimpositions which Colin Rowe, Robert Slutzky, and Bernhard Hoesli have characterized as "phenomenal transparency."[22] The salon, for example, could be described as a hall with a bow window, positioned transversely in relation to the house, like the work room on the street. Thanks to the wide opening, however, its middle is also readable as an extension of the dining room, which terminates only in the concave glass and curtain wall near the conservatory. Or as a part of the projection room between the gallery and the "stage prospect," as described above. The design of the ceiling with its beams reflects this multiple legibility so clearly that it recalls the diagram used by Hoesli to illustrate such transparency phenomena. Here too, the tectonic form is placed at the service of the spatial effect.

---

19 Horta, *Mémoires* (see n. 8), p. 94. The artist Fernand Dubois, a medalist, is said to have come to grief on the unaccustomed scale of the work. On the various attempts at designing the salon, see in particular Hanser, *The Early Works of Victor Horta* (see n. 10), pp. 276–279.
20 This fragment was exposed during the restoration.
21 The sketch, possibly the work of Eugène Broerman, was exposed during the reservation and then repainted. It was not adequately documented. One of the figures may have portrayed Emile Tassel. See Françoise Dierkens-Aubry, "Les débuts de l'Art Nouveau à Bruxelles," in: *Bulletin de la Commission Royale des Monuments et des Sites,* 13 (1986), pp. 7–36, here pp. 17, 26–27.
22 Colin Rowe, Robert Slutzky, *Transparency,* with commentary and an addendum by Bernhard Hoesli, (Basel: Birkhäuser, 1997), 3rd ed., pp. 60–61.

The Hôtel Tassel can be characterized as a sequence of clearly defined rooms that are centered by local symmetries, concave forms, and precise proportions, and which are designed atmospherically in relation to their functions and sequenced according to an orthogonal axial system. This arrangement, which corresponds to the tradition of Beaux Arts architecture, is, however, supplemented and overlaid with diverse and surprising spatial relationships. It is no accident that the first publications of the house display corner views exclusively.[23] Disappearing in them is the rigorous axiality, while transitions between rooms and their openness are emphasized. The result is a complexity that is anchored in the severe and ultimately straightforward disposition. The layout is open, but by no means "free"!

Similarly ambivalent is the use of iron. Horta used rolled sections, wrought iron, and cast-iron elements alongside one another and in all possible combinations. He exploited not just the structural capacities of his material, but also its extreme ductility. It is a question here not of the bundling of loads on the smallest number of supporting points, but instead of the shaping of the loads and the support structure in the service of shaping the space. Horta handles the material not as an engineer or a decorator, but instead as an architect. Or as Julius Meier-Graefe puts it in *Dekorative Kunst*: "He [Horta] is a bold *constructeur,* an architect par excellence who stands far above the decorator […]. Horta's strength is his brilliant disposition of spaces."[24]

Martin Tschanz

---

23 See *L'Emulation* (1895), pls. 39–43; with the same in part redrawn illustrations, in: François Thiébault-Sisson, "L'Art Décoratif en Belgique – Un Novateur: Victor Horta," in: *Art et Décoration,* 1 (1897), pp. 11–18.

24 "Er [Horta] ist ein kühner Konstrukteur, ein Baumeister par excellence, der weit über dem Dekorateur steht […] HORTA's Stärke ist eine glänzende Raumverteilung." Julius Meier-Graefe, "V. Horta," in: *Dekorative Kunst,* vol. 3, no. 5 (1900), pp. 206–209, here p. 206.

2

MAISON DE VERRE   PIERRE CHAREAU

MAISON DE VERRE   PIERRE CHAREAU   38

MAISON DE VERRE   PIERRE CHAREAU   40

Maison de Verre: a "machine pour l'art de vivre"

POETRY OF PROGRESS

A founding member of modern movements such as CIAM and UAM,[1] Pierre Chareau's involvement in the emergence of the French avant-garde of the 1920s is readily apparent. Having grown up in a sophisticated milieu and having spent nearly a decade making a name for himself as an *ensemblier meublier* with designs for interiors prior to his activities as an architect, he was ideally conversant with the social customs and conventions of bourgeois life. As an *ensemblier,* he unified the seemingly divergent poles of avant-garde architecture and traditional interior design, resulting in a distinctive conception of modernity and progress. In contrast to the prevalent themes of rationalization, for instance the abstraction or standardization of construction, central to the Maison de Verre, completed in 1932, instead emphasized the scenographic aspects of modern technology—and at the same time a different way of expressing modernity, i. e. not defined as the technological per se, and instead as a fascinating and sensuous embodiment of progress. In the Maison de Verre, for example, the technically progressive conception of the floor heating was complemented by the straightforward mechanism of a "simple machine"[2] that was based on gravity and set into motion by human power. Although Chareau was indisputably a pioneer in the realm of structural engineering when it came to the deployment of innovative materials such as duraluminium[3] or the daring application of glass bricks[4] on façades, and was emphatically interested in progress, the formal language of technology was nonetheless still coupled

---

1   The UAM (Union des Artistes Modernes) was formed in 1929 with the aim of departing from traditional interior decoration and instead emphasizing the investigation of new materials and technologies in order to attain a modern orientation and revaluation of handicraft work.

2   In physics, the term "simple machine" or "converter" is defined as a mechanical device which alters the point of attack, direction, or magnitude of a variable with the aim of the employing the available power in the fashion most appropriate to the performance of work.

3   Duraluminium was developed as a material for the construction of airships, which is to say for aircraft construction. The Junkers F13, built in 1919, was the first fully metal aircraft in duraluminium.

4   The glass-brick construction of a façade was a bold undertaking, and the firm of St-Gobain refused to provide a manufacturer's guarantee for such an unanticipated and novel application. The client supported Chareau in his vision, waiving the guarantee.

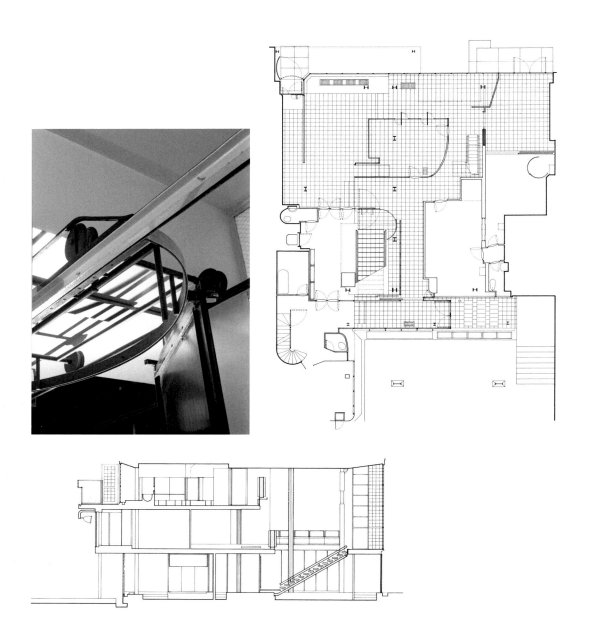

Above left: metalwork, mechanical detail;
above right: floor plan ground floor;
below: section

MAISON DE VERRE   PIERRE CHAREAU   42

to iconographic images of the past.[5] The Maison de Verre is reminiscent of a nostalgic machine whose admirable perfection and haptic qualities entice us to use it. Where technology is not experienced in purely formal terms, but instead also in relation to its sensuous qualities, expressive force, and its pictorial and metaphorical aspects, then the resident—as an element of a scenographic whole—remains a dynamic and active protagonist. Today, when domestic technology tends increasingly toward high-tech and incomprehensible specialization, this approach seems particularly topical: for this reason too, the Maison de Verre appears as a timeless piece of architecture. Through its distinctive expressive force, it positions the human individual at the focus of attention as a responsible actor.

The sensuous and expressive construction of the Maison de Verre is a key to creating a poetry of the everyday—and a catalyst for comfort in steel construction (p. 40). Here, however, poetry as a resource of visualization does not serve to transcend reality, but instead to sensitize us to the beauty of the profane, as a contemporary and friend of Chareau wrote: "Chareau enjoyed discovering beauty in the commonplace. […] I am absolutely convinced that the poet's role is not—as is all too often said—to take us into another world, but quite the opposite—to captivate and us with the charm or to move us with the grandeur of all that we look at day after day, and do not actually see […]."[6]

Another idiosyncrasy in the construction of the Maison de Verre lies in its linguisticality, which Bruno Reichlin has described, with reference to the steel supports of the two-story living room, as "simultaneously an analytical and a descriptive language."[7] Striking in particular alongside the supports, positioned prominently in the space, is the enormous concentration of expression. Heightened haptic qualities and plasticity emerge through the tension between the riveted steel profiles and the smooth surfaces of the slate slabs. This detail also accents the axiality of the profiles and hence the—actually justified in structural terms—rotation of both pillars toward the façade. This

5   On this issue, Bruno Reichlin remarked: "From the point of view of technology, the supports actually belong to the 19th century. In the building that itself as the *non plus ultra* of modernism and has been received as such, the supports clearly reveal their scenographic function. As a technically obsolete solution which will henceforth belong to the familiar iconography of the world of technology (like Stephenson's locomotive, depicted in stylized form on information boards at railway crossings), it is used in order to cajole encounters between the domestic-profane and the machine age." From Wolfgang Schett, Christian Sumi, and Bruno Reichlin, "Analytische versus synthetische Konstruktion" in the article "Architektur und Konstruktion," in: *Werk, Bauen und Wohnen,* 11 (1992), pp. 41–48, here p. 46.

6   René Herbst, *Un inventeur ... l'architecte Pierre Chareau,* with a foreword by Francis Jourdain, Paris: Editions du Salon des Arts Ménagers, 1954, p. 4; foreword by Francis Jourdain reprinted in Marc Vellay, Kenneth Frampton, *Pierre Chareau: Architect and Craftsman, 1883–1950* (New York: Rizzoli, 1990), pp. 29–31, here p. 29.

7   "Chareau's approach to construction could be referred to as analytical: the supports of the Maison de Verre describe all of the elements used as well as its assembly arrangement. This analytical approach amuses itself with the 'exposure' of constructive elements; the supports consist of sheet iron onto which four angle profiles have been bolted; each element is clearly identifiable (the way in which they were drawn from the rolling machine and roughened and trimmed without a welding seam), while the bolts call attention to the doubling at the middle of the support of the assembly. Here, it is a question of a language that is analytical as well as descriptive." Reichlin, "Analytische versus synthetische Konstruktion" (see n. 5), p. 46.

interruption of the linear principle also serves to vary the proportions and scales, setting them in relationship to the space. With the transition from the pillars to the ceiling, the structural function is visualized by a detail (possibly in place of capitals?) with expressive triangular blades. The differentiated red and black coloration calls attention to the inner and outer surfaces of these pillars, which are clad rather than disguised by the slate slabs (p. 38). In accordance with the principle of "core form" and "artform," these measures inscribe a linguisticality into the functional structure of the house, masterfully organizing the various structural members into a complex network of relationships.

A THREE-DIMENSIONAL "PLAN LIBRE"

The way in which Chareau proceeded when producing designs as an *ensemblier meublier* was described by Pierre Migennes in 1932: "It is, first and foremost, about the redisposition and the rearrangement of the space. All the partitions in the old apartment are knocked down to obtain a single room that is as large as possible. Then, into this great empty space, the rooms with all the varying functions that existed before are reinserted in such a way as to retain all of advantages of the newly recovered large space."[8]

Chareau encountered an analogous situation with the "insertion"[9] of the Maison de Verre into the urban context. He achieves the empty, free space by means of a delicate steel structure, together with the self-supporting façade screen, consisting of glass bricks, which brings a maximum of light into the interior while at the same time sheltering the inhabitant's private sphere (p. 36). The apartment was freely inserted into this newly-won space like a stage set. Taking Le Corbusier's *plan libre* to a new level, Chareau develops the independence of function and structure in the third dimension: attained in the integral, interconnected spatial figure of the Maison de Verre is an astonishing spaciousness and a remarkable impression of expansiveness, since spatial boundaries are withdrawn from the gaze, with the rooms overlapping and spatial transitions between them being variable (p. 42). Two-sided cabinets, mobile walls, and even adjustable stairs make it possible to adapt spatial transitions and relationships to the desired degree of privacy as needed or in response to mood (p. 37). This spatial convertibility is continued in the expendable or reducible furniture designs, whose effect on the space differs according to the user situation. Like its construction, the space of the Maison de Verre appears like a kind of machine which can be adjusted as desired and operated in order to continually reformulate the wealth of human relations (p. 46).

---

8   Pierre Migennes, "Sur deux ensembles de P. Chareau," in: *Art et Décoration,* T.LXI, (1932), pp. 129–140; in English in: Vellay and Frampton, *Pierre Chareau* (see n. 6), p. 60

9   Because the uppermost apartment in the existing house could not be altered due to legal stipulations concerning the tenancy, the Maison de Verre had to be adapted not just laterally, but vertically as well.

AWARENESS OF LIFE AND "L'ART DE VIVRE"

"Chareau was alert. Alert to people, to their needs, their aspirations, to what made them tick; he would watch the way they reacted, and listen to the way they spoke and laughed. [...] He was alert to the times, to the world in progress, to new tendencies in thought and dress, to discoveries in the arts, to the movement of people, classes, and society." [10]

Particularly decisive for the wider attitude toward life cultivated by Pierre Chareau—who was a member of the Paris Salon d'Automne [11] as well as the UAM—were performing arts such as dance, theater, and scenography. [12] His fascination with the formalist movement was linked to his knowledge of the etiquette governing cultivated manners and the rules of courtesy, and culminated in the Maison de Verre in the scenarizing of social ritual, which proceeded on the basis of mechanical systems and permeates the entire building. In a way that complements the steel structure, an important role was played in this context by the intricate metalwork, whose ingenious details were perfected to the highest degree through incalculable effort (pp. 42/46). [13] As a consequence of the ingenious placement of the concealed center of gravity, the curving screen at the feet of the main staircase, for example, seems to be moved smoothly by a magic hand (p. 37). Another instance is the construction—seemingly designed with a wink—of the sliding doors, which glide when opened into the field of vision of the neighboring room, signaling to the man of the house that his wife has entered the adjacent boudoir. With preeminent social formalities, a dependence on the worlds of dance and theater is especially evident: a dignified entrance when climbing to the salon above is underscored by the broad main stairs, where the absence of handrails recalls an ascent to a stage and concludes with backlighting. This aspect of inscribed, formalized movement finds its intensification in the doors separating the waiting room from the consulting room, from which the doctor summons his patients: when the door is opened, the sophisticated construction of the recessed, round handle moves along a curving path on the cambered shape of the door, generating a movement that corresponds to a gallant bow.

Regarding the question of the comfort of steel buildings, an interesting approach is to incorporate the human body directly as an experiential level and to link it with the importance of *galanterie* and elegance. And although

10   In 1980, Chareau's attitude toward life was characterized by Nathalie Dombre in a letter to Kenneth Frampton. Cf. Vellay and Frampton, *Pierre Chareau* (see n. 6), p. 22

11   The Société du Salon d'Automne (Paris Autumn Salon) was founded by the French architect Frantz Jourdain; Pierre Chareau joined in 1921. Thanks to his regular participation in the Salon des Artistes décorateurs and the Salon d'Automne, he became well-known as an *ensemblier meublier.*

12   "We were both great music and ballet lovers. I remember seeing Petrouchka [a ballet by Igor Stravinsky, premiered in 1911] three times in one week, and Pierre [...] who'd heard Pelléas [literary opera by Claude Debussy, premiered in Paris in 1902] at least fourteen times [...]. When we gave a party [...], we would often invite dancers, who would perform on our garden, lawn or in the hall." Letter from Dollie Chareau to René Herbst, 1952, in: Vellay and Frampton, *Pierre Chareau* (see n. 6), pp. 24–28, here p. 26. Chareau contributed to films by Marcel L'Herbier, furniture designs for *L'inhumaine* (1924), and was the *chef décorateur* for *Le Vertige* (1926).

13   Responsible for the locksmith work was the middle Smith Louis Dalbet, who devoted himself unreservedly to the task, even living at the building site for a period of three years.

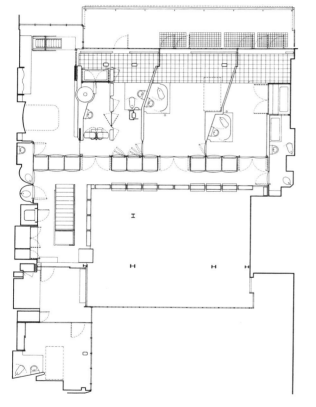

Above left: the private work and relaxation room of the doctor in the first upper story; above right: extendable stairs between the first and second upper stories; lower left: layout of the second upper story; lower right: sanitary facilities with swinging door

MAISON DE VERRE   PIERRE CHAREAU

our present-day attitude toward life is far less characterized by these values, we can nonetheless ask: If elegant movement were to be implemented in the lobby of an apartment building, would the user's attitude toward life be improved, changed, if only for a moment?

MAISON DE VERRE—A SPECIAL "MACHINE À HABITER"

In contrast to the familiar theses of the modern avant-garde, Chareau's design for the Maison de Verre is characterized by the fact that regarding human lifestyles, he assumes no radical break with bourgeois traditions, but on the contrary, recognized the urbane style of life as a fruitful source for his own work. In this consists Chareau's special mastery, which allowed him to inscribe into the building a multilayered network of relationships, as expressed for example via the relationship between core form and art form, or the relationship between individual corporeality and sensory perception and the residential environment. A manifold and lively network of relationships is characteristic of life as such. The architecture of the Maison de Verre is based on this fundamental assumption. When it comes to the comfort of steel buildings, therefore, it may well constitute a fundamental contribution.

Ingrid Burgdorf

My ideas for this article were inspired to a substantial extent by the marvelous guided tour given by Mary Vaughan Johnson, Curator of the Association de la Maison de Verre.

3

EAMES HOUSE   CHARLES & RAY EAMES   48

EAMES HOUSE — CHARLES & RAY EAMES

EAMES HOUSE — CHARLES & RAY EAMES

On the Tectonics of the Eames House

GATEWAY TO THE ATMOSPHERE OF THE 1950S

In at least one respect, the Eames House fits in seamlessly with the other Case Study Houses:[1] all of them convey an atmosphere of lightweight, transparent, and cheerful domesticity—the kind of optimism that was beginning to characterize the lifestyle of the 1950s. Through commercials, household appliances, exhibitions, and magazines, this atmosphere was invoked as the promise of the future, as the "American way of life," and hence elevated to the global standard of existence devoted to carefree fun and self-confidence (p. 54). What has architectural construction contributed to this atmosphere?

In analyses of the Case Study Houses, too little attention has been paid perhaps to the circumstance that the atmosphere of these houses was so to speak "in the air" at the time. The designs and buildings of George Fred Keck,[2] for example, or the early US-American works of Mies van der Rohe, anticipate much that was later explored in the Case Study Houses (p. 54). It seems remarkable that such a lighthearted atmosphere could be conjured to life so soon after a terrible war. By then, however, World War II remained a presence only in the form of armaments-related products such as plastic parts, aircraft glue, and synthetic resins.[3] Undeniably, an almost transparent, cheery lightness is a leitmotif of the Eames House.

THE EAMES HOUSE AS AN INDEPENDENT
INTERPRETATION OF A CASE STUDY HOUSE

Beyond this shared mood, however, the Eames House strikes a very singular architectural tone within the larger corpus of the Case Study Houses. The house conveys the atmosphere of an informal, almost fragile architecture, with the elements painstakingly and almost weightlessly assembled to create an enthralling spatial structure and a powerful sculptural body. Palpably, the design draws its strength from the dialogue between interior and exterior, and

1   Elizabeth A. T. Smith, *Case Study Houses* (Cologne: Taschen, 2009).
2   Georg Fred Keck, 1895–1980, US-American modernist architect from Chicago.
3   Marilyn Neuhart, John Neuhart, *Eames House* (Berlin: Ernst, 1994), p. 18.

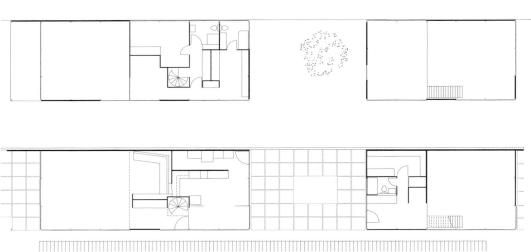

Above left: Steel House (CSH No. 22, 1960), Pierre König;
above right: Green's Ready-Built Homes (1945), George
Fred Keck; below: plans, Eames House

EAMES HOUSE CHARLES & RAY EAMES 54

it seems almost astonishing that this finely balanced site between the slope and the eucalyptus trees was to some extent only the second choice. An earlier scheme projected perpendicular to the slope from the hill. In its delicacy, it is reminiscent of the hovering pavilion houses, celebrations of lightweight qualities, which modernism held in readiness almost as prototypes. Superficially, at least, it appears that the Eames House—as No. 8 in the series—can be integrated effortlessly into the celebrated Case Study series published by the magazine *Arts & Architecture*.[4] A closer inspection, however, reveals that the house is remote from the research conducted through the Case Study Houses project, whose aim was to develop a lightweight steel construction system whose spans made possible the use of strikingly large-scale windowpanes (p. 54). These large panes almost serve as the trademark of the Case Study Houses. Decisive in the Eames House is the opposite: the breaking down of the surfaces of the cube into a network of relatively small fields.

THE COMPOSITE GRID

Case Study No. 8 is first and foremost an investigation of a delicately crafted, finely subdivided cell membrane, and the possibilities—despite all of its transparency—of achieving an astonishingly material, corporeal presence through a tight linear network. As a synthesis, at the same time, the house demonstrates the possibilities of interweaving such a highly refined membrane texture with the interior spaces, according to strict rules. The independent, modern style of the Eames House is evident in the relationship between the inside and the outside: despite a possible initial reading, the house is barely interested in the tectonic and expressive problems of a construction system. Far from allowing the joins of the constructive elements to vanish in sophisticated, predetermined system joints, it on the contrary displays the seams, the joins, between structural members as nodal positions in a fabric of lines and surfaces. At the same time, the additive character of these elements emphasizes the fragility of a light-flooded object. The design of the Eames House is extraordinarily atmosphere-driven, meaning that the syntax is not dominated by the technical solution, but instead by perceptions of the interplay of its material concretizations. The form itself, however, was not Charles Eames's ultimate aim, but instead a "quality," to use his own word, albeit one he never circumscribed more precisely.[5] Arguably, then, this shifts the material properties of the architectural scheme into the foreground.

TRUSCON: A CATALOG OF BUILDING COMPONENTS

Herein lies the distinctive contribution of the Eames House to the history of modern construction. Valid as well for Ray and Charles Eames, certainly, was the maxim "less is more,"[6] but the modernist tendency toward abstraction

---

4   *Arts & Architecture,* US-American architectural magazine published between 1929 and 1967, and under the direction of J. Entenza beginning in 1940. Cf. Smith, *Case Study Houses* (see n. 1).

5   Neuhart and Neuhart, *Eames House* (see n. 3), p. 10.

6   Ibid.

Advertising poster for Truscon steel products

which streamlines tectonics and hence reduces the haptic qualities of the materials is nonetheless foreign to the Eames House.

In this oscillation between abstract geometrical order and material presence, the house is recognizable for its independence: in conformity with the commission of the Case Study Houses, the Eameses use a large number of readily accessible prefabricated construction elements from the production catalog of a large supplier in this field, namely Truscon (p. 56).[7] As envisioned by the Case Study program, House No. 8 was one of eight experimental steel houses.[8] Prefabricated steel presupposes an objective, hardheaded, systematic design strategy, as was evident to the Eameses. But they did not, however, concern themselves with a unified logic of joins, as suggested by these Truscon components—even though these were not actually conceived as a construction system in the narrow sense of the term. The Eameses employed the full available spectrum of trusses, supports, and windows like a construction and building materials directory, and assembled them in such a way that they generally remain recognizable as elements. This is true for many of these standard components, but in particular for the infill panels, for the shed-style window panes, and for the pillars beneath the roof (pp. 50-52). Individual assembly techniques required a kind of bricolage technique, because the connections between the elements had to be invented and fabricated in each individual instance.[9]

THE JOIN AS "HANDICRAFT"

This constructive improvisation extended so far, that some of the connections are said to have been welded together by office colleagues. Handmade adjustment work was undertaken for the basic system parts as well, and with nearly all window frames.[10] Glass sliding doors were constructed individually for specific positions within the grid.[11] Nowhere is the potential of this procedure clearer than in the minute calibration of the widths of the grid outlines on the outside, and therefore the interplay between the dimensions of the glass frames, stanchions, secondary reinforcements, and the frames of the operable windows. Reflected in this materiality of the parts is Charles Eames's statement that he wanted to conceive a network for the shell that

---

7   For the reference to Truscon, as well as for references to a number of other source materials, our thanks to the architect Frank Escher of Escher GuneWardena Architecture Inc., Los Angeles, who was involved in the renovation of the Eames House.

8   Neuhart and Neuhart, *Eames House* (see n. 3), p. 28.

9   Ibid., p. 39.

10   Ibid., pp. 38, 61, 63. On this point, the sources are not free of contradiction. Bojana Banyaz, who worked for GuneWardena Architecture on the restoration, wrote to us, for example: "I don't remember that Eames office members were working on the original construction of the house, rather, on later changes and repairs. There are some oral history documents saved probably in the CMP folder. One of these interviews was with Randy Walker (I think), who did speak about doing repairs later on. But these were all in the 70s. I think all these people would have been too young to work on the original house."

11   Ibid., p. 39. Thanks to the architect Frank Escher for the reference to the custom-made sliding windows.

Above: view, Eames House (drawing based on the illustration in Neuhart and Neuhart, *Eames House* [see n. 3]); middle left: detail view of the façade; middle right: Herman Miller Showroom (1950), Ray and Charles Eames

EAMES HOUSE   CHARLES & RAY EAMES   58

would be simultaneously structural while providing enclosure.[12] For the sake of *gestalt* and also of integrity, such an aim required minimum material weight. Impressive here is the way in which, in this double game, the space-delimiting, highly tensile fabric transmits a sense of stability and movement into the space—with so little material and so much transparency. The importance accorded to this network and to the proportions between its members, is visible already in the elegant, highly graphic plans of the façade. (p. 58).[13] The almost figurative intention behind this construction resonates in the warm, dark anthracite of the painted steel, used both inside and out. "The constant strength of this line" was particularly important to Eames.[14]

PANELS AS WALL SUBSTITUTES

Naturally, the material filling of the panels is accorded an important role, and the closed panel surfaces and glass with varied materiality (wired glass, opaque glass, structured glass) are joined with great precision to the spatial order that lies behind them: to the ceiling, to spatial depth, and to function. In their materiality, wired glass, opaque glass, and plaster panels display their materiality as infills (p. 58). Among the striking peculiarities of this design approach is the dialectic of a tightly meshed configuration of fields that seems free and unconstrained to begin with, yet displays a rigorous, almost functionalistic binding of this configuration to changes of thickness and the function of the spaces on the inside (privacy, intimacy). Exterior and interior, then, are held together by the same gesture: a modern, modular, planar organization which makes the walls visible inside as a space-shaping membrane, and asserts the plastic characteristics of the architectural body on the outside (pp. 49-50). Already the shed-style industrial glazing endows the shell with tremendous fragility. The fact that this effect was achieved only by piecing together the construction elements step by step is confirmed by a letter written by Charles Eames, which asserts that much of the allure of the spaces was the result of ad-hoc decisions and of an unplanned clash of the parts.[15] This trait emerges perhaps particularly clearly in contrast to the elegant Herman Miller Studio (1950) (p. 58), so similar in character, where the glass front, subdivided with mullions, appears more as a curtain than as an attempt to prevent the flow of the space toward the outside through haptic materiality.

PRAGMATIC JOINS

Just how remote the Eames House is from the constructive intentionality and discipline of an architect like Mies van der Rohe becomes clear in the construction of the corners of the building (p. 60). While in the corner of Craig

---

12 Daniel Ostroff, *An Eames Anthology* (New Haven: Yale University Press, 2015), pp. 68–71, point 8 of the letter; C. Eames: "I have thought of our house as a great web which at the same time supports and encloses."

13 Neuhart and Neuhart, *Eames House* (see n. 3), pp. 39, 40, 41.

14 Ibid., p. 43.

15 Ostroff, *An Eames Anthology* (see n. 12), pp. 68–71, point 8 of the letter.

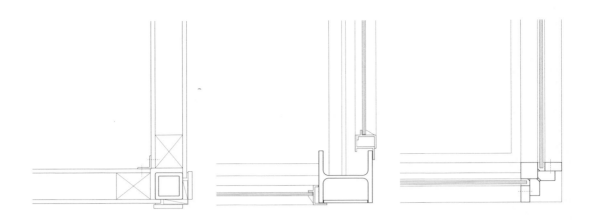
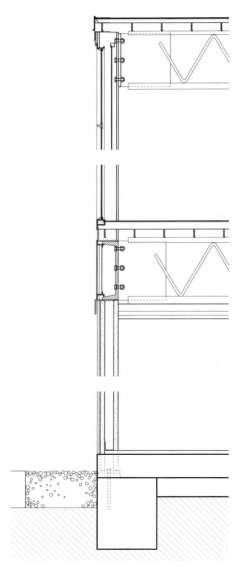

Above: comparison of corner details (from left to right):
CSH No. 18 (1958), Craig Ellwood / Eames House /
Farnsworth House (1951), Ludwig Mies van der Rohe;
below: section, Eames House

Ellwood's House No. 18,[16] for example, a consciousness of the directionally neutral tectonic expression of the Miesian corner is expressed through the minimal recess of the thick retaining plate, such finely chiseled interests are alien to the Eames House. Its corner window details carry the features of the Truscon window frame around the corners and directly onto the H-beams, with the channels welded together in the simplest way. On the inside, where this channel would have left a wide constructive joint, the Eameses inserted a fitted wooden piece, which is painted the same gray color as the steel elements. It may be that this unpretentious directness is the result of their attentive (and well-documented) study of Miesian architecture and the Farnsworth House at the large MoMA exhibition of 1947.[17] With this uncontrived corner detailing, the Eameses perhaps wanted to document their rather pragmatic understanding of technique.

THE MOVEMENT OF THE SPACE

In the interior, through the contrasting effects, the character of this finely calibrated façade skin is particularly evident (p. 51): while the mullions and supports appear almost like thick lines of ink, this play of lines and joins is to some extent counteracted by the closed surfaces, endowing the beautifully dynamic space with foreground, movement, and depth. As documented by photographs, even the curtains participated in a play of reduced transparency. This organization of surfaces through an order of reduced clearness is among the most striking aspects of the material definition of the outer external membrane for the sake of the space. If the house displays aspects of De Stijl construction, then this is not the result of the use of color and line, but instead of the highly striking interior structure. The overhanging upper-story balustrade and the sitting niche endow the main space with a pull into depth along the façade, embedding the eat-in kitchen into the larger structure. The contrary movement of the upper story, where the balustrade is set back in the high space, creates a flowing transition to the bedrooms. The smooth corridor ceiling and the seamless, closed façade elements, the changing room heights together with the tensed surface of the railing constitute these unexpected spatial movements with resources that were developed in modernism beginning with De Stijl in order to transfer the space into the third, the vertical dimension, and to effect spatial flow (p. 50). All of these elements are integrated into the geometry of the principal structure, endowing the interior space with a sense of movement.

COMFORT IN A STEEL HOUSE

In closing, it is worth emphasizing another unexpected interior spatial feature of the finely calibrated, network-style, static grid structure: the elasticity of the absorption of objects and items of furniture as an expression of the

---

16   Smith, *Case Study Houses* (see n. 1), p. 244.
17   Neuhart and Neuhart, *Eames House* (see n. 3), p. 24. Exhibition on the work of Mies van der Rohe in MoMA, New York, 1947, with a catalog by Philip Johnson.

claiming of the space for daily life. Furnishings, personal possessions, works of art and textiles in a sense nestle into the constructive elements, thus overriding the severe regime in the organization of the steel elements (p. 51). This convergence between structure and furnishings becomes especially clear in the use of wood for the large wall and of strong canvas for panel coverings. As items of furnishing and screening elements, curtains and sliding panels endow the grid structure with depth, at the same time emphasizing individual elements through planarity. As Marilyn and John Neuhart argue in their book on the Eames House, it is precisely through the interference between elements of furnishing and the ordered structure that the house assumes the character of an exhibition of the works of Charles and Ray Eames.[18] In an unexpected way, even nature comes close to this exhibition character. The trunks and branches of the massive trees intrude into the interior of the house almost like exhibits (p. 50). Through their contrast with the orthogonal grid structure, the presence of the organic forms is remarkably heightened.

AS FOUND?

Based on the interaction between these various levels of design, we can arrive at the unexpected conclusion that the Eames House is held together far less than one might expect by the constructive syntax of the steel system, but is instead dominated by the interest in the expressive power of modern materials, which is shifted into the foreground by the unprejudiced, free joining of the building parts. This argument was made by *Arts & Architecture*.[19] Asserting itself here very quietly is the "as found" quality of the house, the result of the way in which standard elements and common materials have been, so to speak, collaged together. In the end, the house coheres through the creative attentiveness of its designers, who without reservations trace the formal properties of the rather freely assembled parts. "Most of the qualities that proved satisfying were inherent in the materials themselves—the texture of the ceiling, the metal joists, [...] the change of glazing [...]," commented the Eameses.[20]

Marcel Meili

18   Ibid., p. 8.
19   Ibid., pp. 16, 35.
20   Ibid., p. 37.

CONTEMPORARY STEEL BUILDINGS

1 MÜLLER HOUSE CHRISTIAN KEREZ 2014, ZURICH
Force and Expanse   p. 66

2 53 HLM HOUSES LACATON & VASSAL 2011, SAINT-NAZAIRE
Disarming Lightness   p. 76

3 SCHEEPLOS HOUSE DE VYLDER VINCK TAILLIEU (DVVT) 2011, GHENT
The Everyday and the Avant-Garde   p. 86

4 BRICK LEAF HOUSE JONATHAN WOOLF ARCHITECTS 2003, LONDON
Wolf in Sheep's Clothing   p. 96

5 HOUSE WITH THIN WALLS
MARTIN BÜHLER
2010, ZURICH

Welded Walls   p. 106

6 RUA DO TEATRO
SOUTO DE MOURA
1995, PORTO

Paraphrasing a Building Tradition   p. 116

7 TERRACE HOUSE
ATELIER BOW-WOW
2011, YOKOHAMA

Framing and Filling   p. 126

8 APARTMENT BUILDING
GRASER ARCHITEKTEN
2012, ZURICH

Dressed in Metal   p. 136

9 APPARTEMENT V3
MADE IN
2015, GENEVA

Shimmering Character   p. 146

1

MÜLLER HOUSE   CHRISTIAN KEREZ   66

1   Force and Expanse

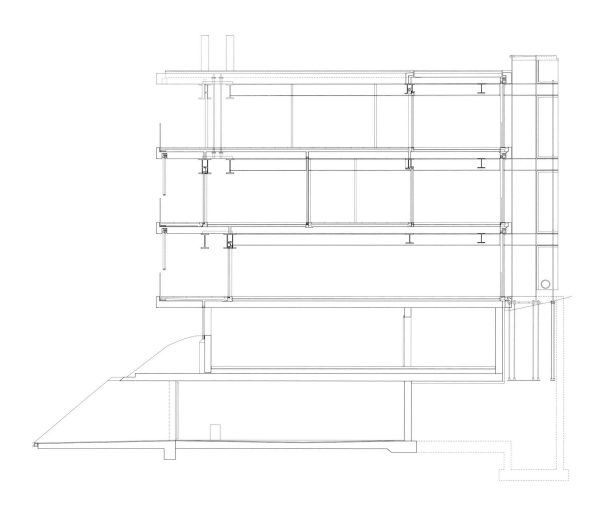

MÜLLER HOUSE   CHRISTIAN KEREZ

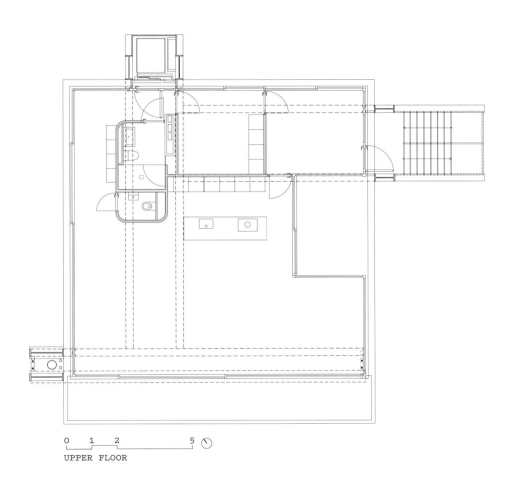
UPPER FLOOR

SPATIAL TEST ARRANGEMENTS

With the architecture of Christian Kerez, it is a question not so much of comfort or utility, but instead of a confrontation with fundamental questions about space.[1] Each project can be regarded as a specific experimental test arrangement, which emerges from a dialogue with Joseph Schwartz and which strives toward a unity of "material, construction, and space-shaping support structure." Accorded priority, then, is space and its relationship to structure, and the constructive materialization is the logical result of these concerns.[2]

The free play of the space and the appearance of functional and constructive elements furnishes the conceptual point of departure for the Müller House on the hillside above Zurich. All structural verticals such as supports, stairs, elevator, and shafts have been banished from the interior, resulting in loft-style spaces, glazed on all sides, on each of the three levels. That this also entails the displacement of the vertical load transfer from the isolation perimeter and the vast cantilevers constitutes the self-imposed constructive challenge, which can only be confronted with steel.

A similar initial situation was present already with the House with Lake View in Thalwil, whose freely configured interior develops in linear fashion via a terrace-style staggered arrangement toward a framed view of the landscape. In the Müller House, however, the view of Lake Zurich opens up instead diagonally via the corners of the building. Only from the uppermost story do we really gaze past the environs, contemplating the lake and the city in all of its beguiling vastness. The Müller House, then, goes one step further: on the southwestern corner, which is somewhat neuralgic when it comes to views, supports are renounced entirely (p. 74).

IN A POWERFUL, NAKED SPATIAL VOLUME

The entrance to the house is dramaturgically disconcerting. Through a garage door, we pass elegant automobiles to arrive at a fire door with an elevator, which carries the visitor up into the interspace that is contained by one of the three externally positioned pairs of steel slabs (p. 75). Crossing the threshold, we pass into the entry area of the apartment on the sloping side, and are confronted there directly and in a highly confined space with the tension between the massive structure and the transparent façade.

In the apartment, the nearly black cantilevers—through their dimensions, those of bridge construction, and through their doubling as a pair of girders—appear colossal in this residential environment. In their forcefulness, they unavoidably condition our perception of the space, which, however, reveals itself via movement to be quite multifaceted.[3] At first, one feels almost crushed by the density of the pair of girders. When viewing the inner façade frontally, they give the beholder a sense of remoteness from the surroundings, despite the greatest possible transparency of the glazing. They frame an image and at the same time seem to hold the view of the outside at a distance (p. 67). In a sense, the heavy, protruding construction forms a protective spatial volume that makes the experience of being put on display endurable, even with maximal glazing. At times, effects of mirroring and reflection are superimposed on the external elements of the construction, so that even the massive pairs of steel slabs are barely perceptible within the interior. In the neuralgic southwest corner, the girders guide the gaze past the town and into the far distance (p. 74).

TO PUSH THE BOUNDARIES OF THE POSSIBLE A BIT FURTHER

The mystical aspect of the project is conditioned not least of all by its structural complexity, which is realizable only with difficulty in relation to a house with three apartments.[4] The support structure has been inserted below into a concrete pedestal, which, however, barely makes an appearance in contrast to the steel towers and the floor slabs. The gallows-shaped frames span the orthogonal volumes on three sides, coming into contact with one another. Six cantilever arms measuring between 12 and 14 meters in length are friction locked on the exterior to the gallows slabs, ensuring the overall stability of the building (p. 72).

In a recent collection of essays addressing the dialogue among "les constructeurs" (*Dialog der Konstrukteure*),[5] Joseph Schwartz characterizes the enormous potential of prestressing, which makes it possible to control deformations to the greatest extent despite significant overhangs. The "feel for internal forces," and a knowledge of the reciprocal interaction between tension and compression forces within a system, also facilitates the thermally separated force transmission in the area of the façade. This building demonstrates that the boundaries of the possible can be displaced just a bit further (p. 74).[6]

Beyond the structural system itself, a global understanding of these relationships makes possible an innovative fire-protection concept. The fulfillment of the requirements of serviceability determines the dimensioning of the cantilevers, so that these exhibit reserves with regard to carrying capacity. In combination with the concrete floor slabs, this structural potential can be activated for fire protection, so that the necessary fire resistance is attained. This not only elevates the efficiency of the supporting structure, but also makes possible the renunciation of fire-protection coatings on supports in the interior. The steel remains unprotected, and corresponds in its directness and forcefulness to the archaic spatial conception.

Tanja Reimer

Architecture: Christian Kerez, Werner Schührer, Hannes Oswald, Lukas Ingold
Supporting structure: Dr. Schwartz Consulting, Joseph Schwartz, Neven Kostic
Building physics: Bakus Bauphysik
Fire safety: Mario Fontana

1   "It [the architecture] is in a sense an artform in a perpetual predicament, threatened on its own terrain of three-dimensional, accessible space with being unable to say anything new, of falling silent. The impetus, then, is to break away from all of these constraints and expectations, in order to arrive once again at architecture, to create spaces that can be understood and experienced first and foremost as architectonic manifestations." Hubertus Adam, Christian Kerez, "Die existenzielle Dimension der Architektur," in: Marc Angélil, Jörg Himmelreich, Departement für Architektur der ETH Zürich (eds.), *Architekturdialoge: Positionen – Konzepte – Visionen,* (Sulgen: Niggli, 2011), pp. 488–501.

2   Christian Kerez, "Architektur als Entität von Material, Konstruktion und raumbildender Tragstruktur," in: Aita Flury (ed.), *Dialog der Konstrukteure* (Sulgen: Niggli, 2011), pp. 121–124.

3   "I am more preoccupied with the space-shaping attributes of an architectonic element than with its material appearance or structural performance. Each architectonic elements, wall or support, contributes to shaping the space. In order to emphasize this character, I attempt to reduce these elements in the individual projects, while positioning them clearly in relationship to one another." Tibor Joanelly, "Skulpturale Studien. Werkstattgespräch mit Christian Kerez," in: *Schweizer Ingenieur und Architekt,* no. 4, (2000), pp. 56–60, here p. 57.

4   Through the question of proportionality and the renunciation of any reference to the context, the house has a polarizing impact, and has instigated— albeit indirectly—a cultural-political discussion. See Tibor Joanelly, "Schwebe-Experiment: Haus an der Krönleinstrasse von Christian Kerez," in: *Werk, Bauen und Wohnen,* 1/2 (2015), pp. 66–69; and Hubertus Adam, "Verstörend radikal," in: *Tec 21,* no. 11 (2015), pp. 30–32.

5   Joseph Schwartz, "Gefühl für die inneren Kräfte und die Verhältnismässigkeit zwischen konzeptionellem Denken und Berechnung," in: Flury, *Dialog der Konstrukteure* (see n. 2), pp. 115–119.

6   The following text describes the structural concept in detail and serves as an important source of information: Thomas Ekwall, "Ballett der Kräfte," in: *Tec 21,* no. 11 (2015), pp. 27–30. In addition, Neven Kostic has generously made himself available for questions regarding the supporting structure.

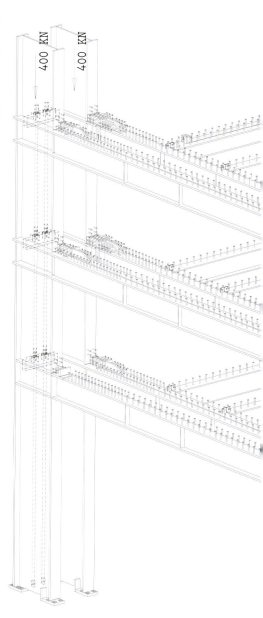

PRESTRESSING

In the freely cantilevering corners, two thin rods testify to the play of forces and to a complex construction process. The prefabricated pillars and beams were prestressed regarding torsion and reversed curving. On the building site, the pairs of supports were positioned with tie rods and finally the pairs of girders assembled story-wise with a superelevation of up to 12 centimeters. After about three weeks, the supporting structure stood "naked" for a moment on the slope. Adjustments were carried out after the concreting of the partially prestressed floor slabs. The prestressing of the tie rods in the southwest corner facilitated the calibration of the façade, so that, after the introduction of all of the dead and live loads, the tensile forces are diminished and the system stabilized. After fine adjustments, the recesses for the prestressing of the floors are closed again and vanish underneath the footfall sound insulation. Nonetheless, the feat achieved by the supporting structure remains palpable upon closer inspection.

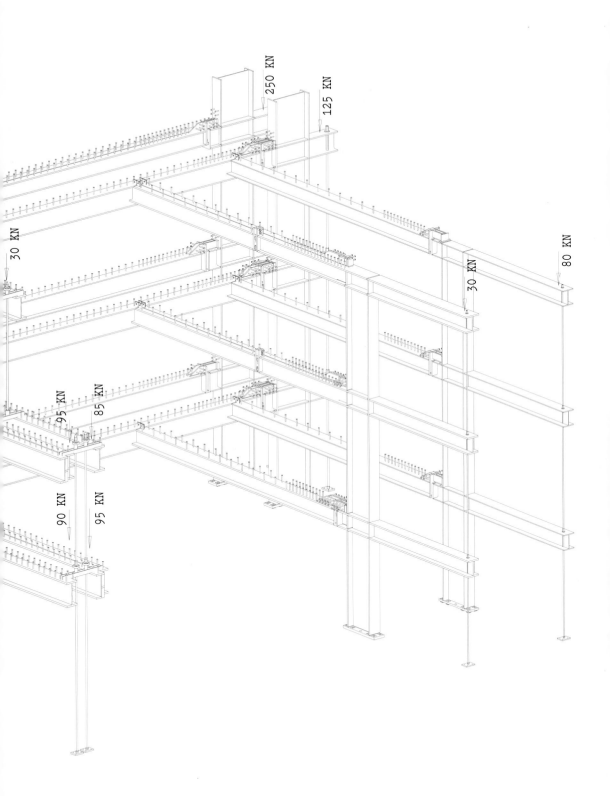

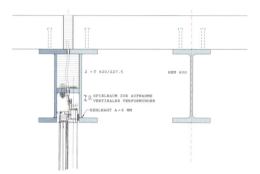
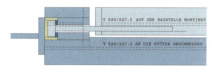
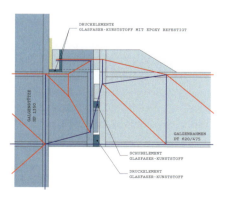

THE DISSOLVING OF FORCES AND BOUNDARIES

The uninterrupted horizontal framing of the view, in conjunction with extreme overhangs, called for constructive research: despite enormous bending torque and shearing forces, no direct contact between steel and steel can be allowed to occur in the area of the insulating perimeter. Pressure and insulating elements in glass-fiber reinforced plastic having the same fire-resistance requirements as steel therefore transfer the forces from the supports to the pillars, simultaneously functioning as spacers and insulation. A supplementary element with higher fire resistance ensures load-bearing capacity in the event the pressure element fails during a fire. The complex nodes, finally, disappear into the concrete ceiling, which meets the façade uncompromisingly. For thermal separation of the girders in the lengthwise direction, the HEM profile is replaced by two welded special profiles, and the façade in between integrated. The overhang in the insulating perimeter, with interpenetrations in the transverse and lengthwise directions, culminates in a multiplicity of different details. Only through an interdisciplinary collaboration between architecture, engineering, building physics, and fire protection could this architectonic concept achieve realization.

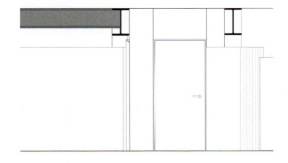

CONSTRUCTED CONTEXT
While the interior benefits from the views, the correlation of the external appearance of the building to its surroundings is consciously bypassed. In the context of individualized apartments, the stairs have lost their functional significance. As a pure escape route, they run directly past the bedroom within the northwestern pair of slabs. Suspended from the girders using thin steel cables, they are fascinating by virtue of their lightweight quality.

INTERIOR
Remaining beneath the girders, which measure 60 centimeters in height, is a clear room height of 2 meters. Despite this openness, the stepped ceiling articulates distinct areas within the space. Functional requirements, such as the separation of sanitary facilities or bedrooms, are handled in a seemingly negligent manner. The necessary installations undermine the structure, and the interfaces are to some extent inserted in a handicraft way, so that when initially occupied, or even after renovation or conversion, the house resembles a spatial sculpture not conceived for habitation. Nonetheless, the compact yet well-proportioned space can be furnished astonishingly well. It offers a powerful aura, and presents occupants with a challenge.

2

53 HLM HOUSES   LACATON & VASSAL   76

2   Disarming Lightness

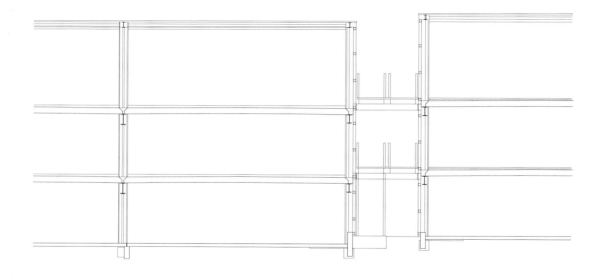

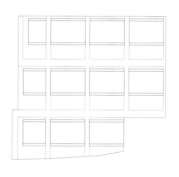

53 HLM HOUSES   LACATON & VASSAL

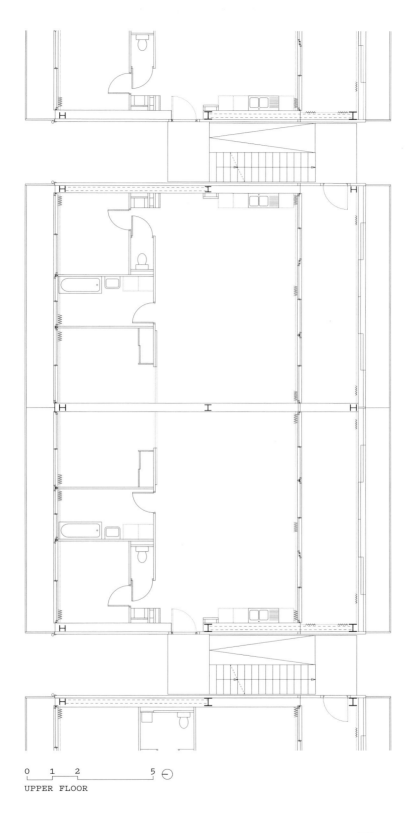

UPPER FLOOR

LIGHT AND AIR

Airy, light-flooded building volumes characterize the housing estate in Saint-Nazaire, a town in the Pays de la Loire region near the Atlantic coastline. Together with the glass fronts and curtains set behind them, delicate aluminum frames spanned with polycarbonate panels generate a perplexing impression, one remote from the solid wall and its boundary function, which these architects consistently call into question: "With the walls, one comprehends the degree to which a dwelling is continually trapped in the logic of protection and isolation, and how deeply defensive is its attitude toward its surroundings."[1] The mobile, lightweight materials of the 53 apartments convey an impression of possibility, of variation, of flexibility. An undogmatic way of life seems to flourish here, where the architecture generates a space with which occupants can "play," and which they can appropriate (p. 77).

STEEL RARELY APPEARS ALONE

However, what conditions are concealed by this architectural impression, which so brazenly flouts European conventions of residence? The project's expression is a retort to the narrow budget corset imposed by the housing subsidy program HLM.[2] Following their studies, Lacaton & Vassal spent a number of years in Niger, and are able to use this invaluable experience to their advantage when dealing with precarious financial constraints.[3] By perfecting the construction, they generate freedom within this straitjacket, as summarized here: "By optimizing construction costs, Lacaton & Vassal are able to modify this equation so that a minimal budget can translate into maximal space."[4]

The objective of lowered building costs and the creation of the maximal space is achieved by a composition that uses diverse materials, which satisfies structural demands directly and, without additional finishes, avoids degenerating into a banal assembly, instead allowing the complex as a whole to develop a sense of identity. The potential of steel lies in the material's pragmatic and materially-appropriate utilization. Here, however, steel requires allies that can compensate for its weaknesses. Only in this way can its economic advantages be exploited.

This phenomenon can be described with reference to the floor slabs (p. 83). It is well-known that in multistory buildings, a minimal steel mass leads to acoustic challenges. One response is to construct the floor slabs from prefabricated concrete elements. The rhythm of prefabrication steel, which sets the tone, is not affected, and acoustic challenges are solved. The building need not be organized around an expensive, space-forming steel skeleton. On the contrary, the steel skeleton does not—as is generally the case—span the building volumes; it is situated in alleyways between the buildings in reduced form, where the neuralgic location fulfills multiple tasks at the same time. On the longitudinal side, girders form the supports for the floor slabs, not unlike a shelving system with shelf boards. In the transverse direction, frames form the supports for cost-effective accesses to the outdoor space, with the weather-resistant properties of galvanized steel being almost celebrated.

The accomplishment of this construction lies in the conscious use of hybrid design methods. Here, the architects must resist the temptations of intellectual systems approaches while compensating skillfully for the consequences of this economically conditioned strategy. This latter occurs in the façade, for example, where the cantilever of the non-loadbearing conservatories and balconies creates the impression of an elegant, delicate steel construction that artfully covers up the internal constructive principle in favor of a powerful image (p. 82).

LIGHT ENTERS, STEEL REMAINS OUTSIDE

In this strategy, light is accorded a special role. It is the central component of a system of values through which architectural quality and economy are renegotiated with the aim of generating added value for residents. The polycarbonate paneling of the movable partition walls of the conservatories refract the light in such a way that they create a textile impression, evoking the archaic in astonishing ways—roughly comparable to the tent structures of the North American native inhabitants, whose scraped leather membranes became so thin that they were light-permeable.[5] On the interior, the steel is perceptible haptically only with structural exceptions, i. e. in the area where it supports the concrete ceiling elements. Clad in fire-protection coatings or plaster, the structural components are deprived of spatial presence, since they merge with a background that has the same color (p. 85). Here, it becomes clear that the internal shell structure primarily fulfills the conditions of an economical space-formation. Its presence of authentic, unfinished surfaces in the living room derives from the use of materials within which steel and concrete are valued higher than plaster or paint. The final appearance does not appear unfinished, but instead belongs to an overarching way of thinking. The structure makes a decisive contribution to the development of a steel atmosphere within. It facilitates large openings, creating a visual link between the interior of the apartment and the atmospherically charged, delicately constructed conservatory. Consequently, the "cozy" aspect of the steel makes itself felt in the living space only indirectly. Solely the dissolution of the wall—made possible by the building shell—allows these external atmospheric factors to become perceptible on the interior (p. 84).

LOW-TECH

An interest in dwellings with varied climate zones that can be linked flexibly with one another makes steel—as a lightweight construction material—indispensable, and demonstrates one of its qualities when applied to residential construction. Given its substantial evaluation, the knowledge transfer of this low-tech strategy into the local culture—where increasingly, demanding residential requirements are often driven ad absurdum by increasing regulatory density—presupposes an intensive collaboration between all project participants. Only in this way can the potential of the residents be reactivated as an integral component within the field of tension between climate, space, and construction (p. 84).

Patric Furrer

Architecture: Lacaton & Vassal
Supporting structure: DIGUET, CESMA, AREA
Metal/steel construction: Ateliers David

1 Jean-Philippe Vassal, Andreas Ruby, "Séjourner sur l'herbe: Zum Technologietransfer von Lacaton & Vassal," in: *Werk, Bauen und Wohnen,* 4 (2002), pp. 10–15, here p. 12.
2 Habitation à loyer modéré.
3 See Nathalie Janson, "Lacaton & Vassal Architects: Learning from Africa," in: Ilka Ruby, Andreas Ruby (eds.), *University Building in France* (Zurich: Holcim Foundation, 2011), p. 74.
4 Nathalie Janson, "No room for standards in sustainable construction," in: ibid., p. 66.
5 Cf. Franziska Leeb et al. (eds.), *Walter Zschokke: Texte* (Zurich: Park Books, 2013), p. 159.

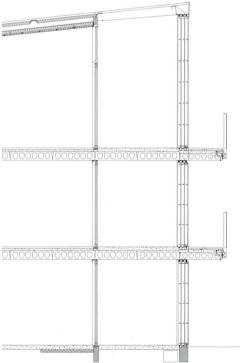

CLAD IN PRINCIPLE

"In contrast, we understand architecture as the layering of clothing on the body. When it's warm outside, you wear a light shirt. When it's somewhat cooler, you wear a pullover on top."[6] But how, in concrete terms, is this promising metaphor to the implemented architecturally? In this region, with its long seasonal transitions and low temperatures, the conservatory is highly efficient as a buffer. In Switzerland, unheated conservatories having surface areas of up to 10 percent of the net floor area are not counted as utilizable space.[7] Despite advantageous legal rulings, conservatories are not widespread in social or cooperative residential developments. Their effectiveness is essentially a question of impermeability. This presupposes high building costs, which are uneconomical in this context. Accordingly, the conservatories in Saint-Nazaire are less effective. In relationship to production costs, however, they do in fact perform well.

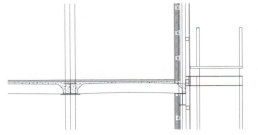

CONCRETE TRAY

Spanned using standardized, pre-stressed, commercially available floor-slab elements are support-free surfaces measuring up to 14.5 × 9 meters, thereby doing justice to a variety of lifestyles. "Rather than being imprisoned in room cells, various functions are able to 'take a walk' through the space, so to speak,"[8] says Jean-Philippe Vassal about open floor plans and the expansion of the house via greenhouse structures. At first glance, the industrial ceilings appear somewhat unconventional. Recognizable only upon closer inspection is the potential of the joins, which orient the space, endowing it with a sense of scale. In this way, the construction becomes architecturally comprehensible for occupants, building a sense of familiarity and trust. But the ceilings are not practical in every respect—the mounting of ceiling lights, for example, becomes impossible, which is a possible drawback for residents.

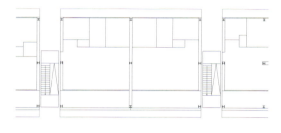

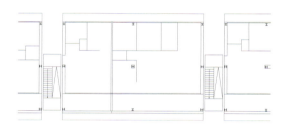

INSULATING CURTAINS

"Isotiss" curtains, consisting of a multilayered, reflective insulating material, are employed in the residential projects of Lacaton & Vassal in a special fashion, and thus could be further developed. They offer residents an additional instrument for regulating comfort: In wintertime, they keep out the cold and reflect thermal radiation into the rooms. In summertime, they prevent the overheating of rooms via thermal emission. In Switzerland, triple glazing is prevalent due to its excellent thermal insulation. The degree of energy transmission however is minimal, so that only circa 45 percent of solar energy streams into the heated room. Handled skillfully, the combination of double glazing and heat-insulating curtains is an efficient approach, since it then becomes possible to respond specifically and hence effectively to the climate situation.

FIRE SAFETY

The efficiency of steel as a construction material is difficult to dispute. "L'inconvénient de l'acier est la protection au feu"[9]—fire safety, as Anne Lacaton points out, is the other side of the coin. How can a pragmatic approach be found while preserving a sense of identity and expression in steel construction? In France, with a building of this height and use, the vertical supporting elements as well as the space-shaping elements must have a fire resistance class of F30.[10] In Saint-Nazaire, the supports are for the most part concealed in crosswall construction, where they are insulated and clad with plasterboard. Only in the apartments, where—due to the sizes of the rooms—the dividing wall is not congruent with the steel structure, must freestanding supports be given a fire-protection coating. The solution lies in the early coordination of spatial program, structure, and fire protection.

6 Vassal and Ruby, "Séjourner sur l'herbe" (see n. 1), p. 13.
7 Cf. reference work of the Canton of Zurich on energetic building regulations: AWEL (Amt für Abfall, Wasser, Energie und Luft), *Vollzugsordner Energie,* 2009.
8 Vassal and Ruby, "Séjourner sur l'herbe" (see n. 1), p. 13.
9 Email from Anne Lacaton, Nov. 11, 2015.
10 Ibid.

3

SCHEEPLOS HOUSE   DVVT

3 The Everyday and the Avant-Garde

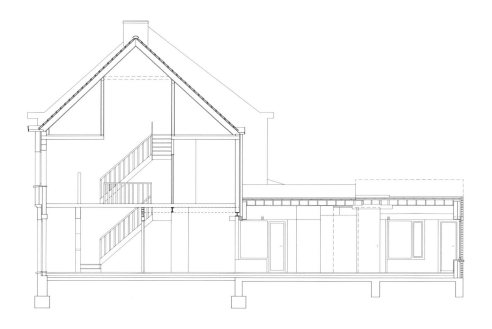

SCHEEPLOS HOUSE   DVVT

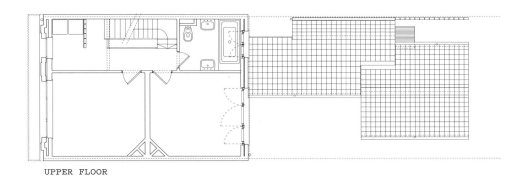

UPPER FLOOR

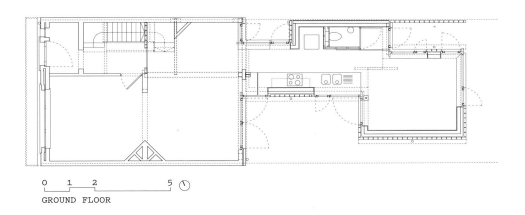

0 1 2   5

GROUND FLOOR

TRANSFORMING ROW HOUSES

As a type of dwelling, the Flemish row house shapes the morphology of the region, along with the personal lives of the inhabitants. Approximately three-quarters of the Flemish population live in private homes, and a large proportion of them are proud owners of row houses.[1] As a rule, this type consists of a front house with adjoining backrooms, the latter often unregulated do-it-yourself buildings that reflect the diversity of reality: here, the heterogeneity of society is reflected in equally non-unified styles of building.[2] In this context, steel as a construction material lends itself to adaptations to the structural system.

In the text "Belgian Architecture as Commonplace: The Absence of an Architectonic Culture as a Challenge" (1987), Geert Bekaert identifies a Belgian culture of building which, anchored in private life, seems difficult to comprehend.[3] Precisely this furnishes the point of departure for the transformations of De Vylder Vinck Taillieu:[4] their attitude and their language are fed by the normality of everyday life, breaking with it on the other hand in order to introduce avant-garde architecture into the private residential environment. Emerging in conventional row houses in this way through dialogue with clients, and often with minimal budgets, are unconventional living spaces.[5]

ANALYTICAL EXPOSURE AND CONSTRUCTIVE ASSEMBLAGE

The Scheeplos House was to have acquired a new kitchen and a spacious dining room—nothing more.[6] Layout studies by the architects document their search for a suitable depth for the intervention and the right relationship between front house and annex.

From the outside, the new backroom appears well integrated into the neighborhood. The bright red brick was the trademark of conversions already in the 1950s and 1960s.[7] Only minor details suggest that the construction is deliberate rather than informal. The lintels of the brick shell are wood, as are the windows, which wrap around the corners—no simple solution, no standard products. Only at first glance does the geometry of the two interpenetrating volumes that form the outdoor spaces appear accidental. The view from the garden onto the small back house with gable displays a respect for the context, but also an inherent irony (p. 92).

Within, the pre-existing front house is altered only in a restrained way. Two steel girders open up the façade to the new spatial sequence, providing an almost literal image on the ceiling of the division of rooms found above. In such cases, the steel would normally be clad; here it is painted apple-green. While all of the other materials in the house have been left in a natural state, here is an instance of staging (p. 93). The steel profiles in the project Les Ballets C de la B were given the same green tone. In the works De Vylder Vinck Taillieu, the color of the steel seems to play a semantic role. Coatings, whether to protect from corrosion or heat, are a constructive characteristic of steel. Aldo Rossi already emphasized steel within the material structure as a conspicuous green element, which complements the red brick of the façade—an instance being the apartment building on Wilhelmstrasse in Berlin. Already green, if less garish, were the painted cast-iron structural elements used by Victor Horta or Henri Labrouste. Is green perhaps the "natural" color of steel?

Manifesting itself in the new dining room with kitchen is a kind of "wild thinking."[8] Supporting and load components appear as elements of an assemblage whose motif is scenic in character (p. 87).

"Construction is something to celebrate in our work but not because it's constructive." This is Jan De Vylder's characterization of the office's attitude toward questions of tectonics.[9] Elements that as a rule remain in the background emerge now into prominence, others are concealed. Concrete, masonry, wood, and steel complement one another in structural terms, as well as atmospherically. This seems reminiscent of the space-shaping "theater of tectonics"[10] found in the works of Victor Horta.

The thin, rounded steel columns with angled supporting brackets are positioned according to spatial criteria, and hence used primarily as accents. The white plaster-clad surfaces expose various material fragments. Through volumetric incisions and views toward the outside, the façade surfaces too participate in this spectacle. A strip of wood marks the complex geometry of the intersecting roof surfaces, thereby emphasizing the transition to the dining room while at the same time quite pragmatically holding the plaster cladding. The expressive color and material deployment of concrete, brick, wood, steel, and plaster allow the construction to appear somewhat surreal, while allusions to the directness of do-it-yourself building are translated now into a creative architectural act (p. 94).

Emerging now where the family gathers is a scenic stage-setting and a total antisystemic but also harmonious and uplifting atmosphere for ebullient everyday life: the space becomes homey. "I can understand that one morning you are in this dining room looking around and you like to understand how it all works. The other morning you give it up and you just enjoy it."[11]

Transcending the division between the front house and annex, finally, the Scheeplos House coalesces now to form a unified whole (p. 92). The conventional row house remains, yet is at the same time significantly altered. Steel makes a small yet indispensable contribution.

Tanja Reimer

Architecture: De Vylder Vinck Taillieu, Dawid Strebicki, Sebastian Skovsted, Sander Rutgers
Supporting structure: Arthur De Roover Structureel Ontwerp

1   See Luise Rellensmann, "Belgien: Backsteine im Bauch," in: *Baunetzwoche,* 356 (2014), http://www.baunetz.de/baunetzwoche/baunetzwoche_ausgabe_3489177.html (last accessed May 15, 2019).
2   See Tom Avermate, "Auf der Suche nach einer genuinen Moderne: Ein begrifflicher Horizont für die Architektur in Flandern," in: *Arch+,* 220 (2015), pp. 10–15.
3   Geert Bekaert, "Belgian Architecture as Commonplace: The Absence of an Architectonic Culture as a Challenge," in: Christophe Van Gerrewey (ed.), *Rooted in the Real: Writings on Architecture by Geert Bekaert* (Ghent: WZW Editions & Productions, Ghent University, 2011), pp. 90–96.
4   Cf. Jan De Vylder on the idea of transformation rather than on distinguishing between a (new) building and conversion, in: Jan De Vylder, "Occasion: Fünf Aphorismen und sieben Umbauten von De Vylder Vinck Taillieu," in: *Werk, Bauen und Wohnen,* 9–2015, pp. 10–15.
5   See architecten de vylder vinck taillieu, Linda Lackner, "de vylder vinck taillieu, Kavel Projekte," in: Arch+, 220 (2015), p. 72.
6   See documentation on the Scheeplos House in: *A + U,* 515 (2013): *Houses by Emerging Architects,* p. 38.
7   Rellensmann, "Belgien: Backsteine im Bauch" (see n. 1).
8   Paul Vermeulen, "Wildes Denken: Die Architektur von De Vylder Vinck Taillieu," in: *Werk, Bauen und Wohnen,* 7/8 (2001), pp. 27–31.
9   Jan De Vylder in the lecture "it does it doesn't," summer workshop "Re-Domesticizing Steel", ZHAW, Winterthur, September 5, 2015.
10 See Martin Tschanz, "Iron in a Not Entirely Bourgeois Residence," in the present publication (p. 27).
11 De Vylder, "it does it doesn't" (see n. 9).

APPROPRIATING NORMALITY

We enter the house through an archway, a motif that is—as a decorative element—anchored in the 1950s. In the most natural way, the diamond pattern of the flooring flows over into the contemporary annex. The addition encompasses a dining room, a kitchen with eight elements, and a restroom—a conventional program. The architecture respects the building task and integrates functional requirements into an expressive spatial composition. A dialogue with the personal needs of the client becomes a form-shaping force.

LOAD AND SUPPORT

The steel girders in the living room depict the room divisions found above. In this way, loads are underpinned in a conventional fashion. They are, however, transferred conceptually: a cruciform support demarcates the orthogonal convergence between the two HEB girders (HEB 160) and the transition from front to back house. The cross, however, is composed of unequal members, and it serves simultaneously—and ambivalently—as a boundary and a connecting element. On the side of the front house, three wings form a T-shaped concrete support on which the steel girders lie. The concrete rim in the annex lies on the fourth member, which is built up as a cross bond of two bricks. In constructive terms, less masonry is hardly possible. The steel lies on concrete, concrete lies on masonry: the change of materials thematizes transition and raises the gable spatially, allowing the annex to seem more complex and larger than it actually is.

CONSTRUCTION AS ACCENT

The concrete gable rests on a green rod with an angle-shaped support—as though it sat in the palm of a hand. Does this piece really have any structural significance? With diameters measuring only 5 centimeters, the dimensioning of the wooden support is reminiscent of a pipe rather than a loadbearing element. It is aligned precisely at the junction of window sash and window frame, to the left of the center of the gable, and hence not at the corner, where the load of the concreted rim arrives. In this situation, another wooden support projects from the corner window. Shifted diagonally in space, at the corner of the small patio of the kitchen, the open corner is dealt with exclusively in wood—no steel. Does the wood support the concrete there? The steel girders single out the dining room and enrich it atmospherically—independently of structural questions, this appears to be their most important function.

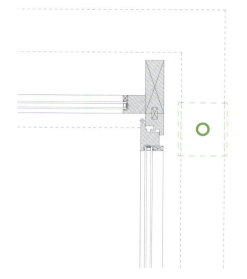

95

4

BRICK LEAF HOUSE

JONATHAN WOOLF
ARCHITECTS

4   Wolf in Sheep's Clothing

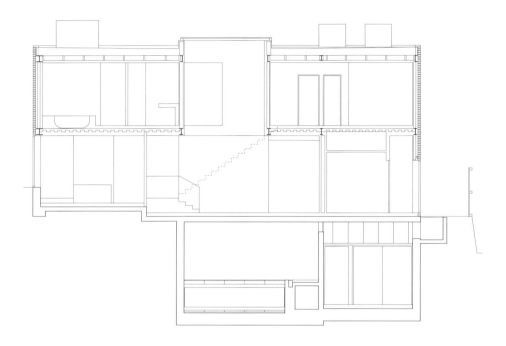

BRICK LEAF HOUSE   JONATHAN WOOLF ARCHITECTS

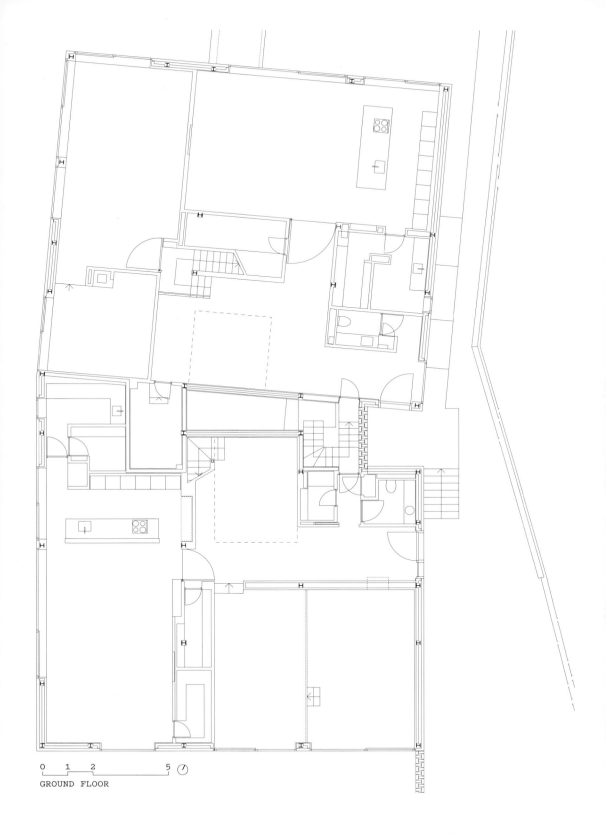

THE CULTURE OF BUILDING IN STEEL

Building in steel is a constructive process that begins already during the design phase, and it confronts planners early on with questions related to span widths, intervals between supports, and issues of assembly. A structural grid must be given consideration from the beginning—at least according to the constructive credo of steel construction in Switzerland. In England, the approach is far more pragmatic: the tradition of building in steel that is rooted there, along with a wide range of supplied systems and solutions offered by contractors, ensures that steel finds broad application. Planners and contractors are quite familiar with hybrid construction. Remote now from tectonic demands, the use of concealed steel favors an unconstrained approach to dealing with the material. The Brick Leaf House demonstrates in an exemplary way how steel need not be visible in order to achieve a visual presence, and that even in the background it can assume a vital role.

APPARENT HEAVINESS

At first glance, the Brick Leaf House appears heavy and solid—an impression that is a function of the homogenous materialization of the façade and the sculptural design language. The volumetric adaptation of the house to the topography results in an incisively molded form that possesses enormous strength (pp. 96-97). Produced in the interior as well is a seeming heaviness, with the concealing plasterboard and façade stanchions making a more voluminous appearance than is actually demanded by structural requirements (p. 105). Only an attentive deciphering of the façade reveals that the house is based on lightweight steel construction. The freely staggered, wide spans of the façade openings, for example, do not correspond to the logic of building in brick; the edges of the floor slabs appear too slender for solid construction; the expansion joints in the façade call attention to the circumferential steel brackets.

Since Jonathan Woolf began by conceiving this two-family house in terms of spatial and atmospheric criteria, the construction played a subordinate role during the initial design phase. Originally, according the architect, he envisioned a solid construction in brick. In the course of project research, however, his attention was drawn to the Krefeld villas of Mies van der Rohe.[1] He characterizes his viewing of them as a decisive experience for the choice of building method. During his visit, the villas were undergoing restoration: the exposed wall construction revealed some of the steel supports which carry the brick façades and ceilings. In an interview, Woolf recalls his astonishment at the time over the pragmatic way in which Mies used steel, and the compromises he was willing to make in the context of a brick building.[2]

Familiar in Switzerland as well are instances of the use of concealed steel: in the 1930s, Artaria & Schmidt built numerous single- and multi-unit homes, whose appearance, both inside and outside, is homogenous.[3] In the context of *Neues Bauen,* their intentions were oriented toward an industrial and economical approach to building. More recent examples as well, such as the Vogesen school building in Basel, built by Diener & Diener, exploit the advantages of steel construction in order to accelerate the building schedule of a structure with its nonetheless stone-like appearance.[4] Conditioned by budgetary considerations, the concealed steel construction remains imperceptible in relation to the building's overall appearance. With the Brick Leaf House, the industrial steel construction method offered the architect astonishing freedom in realizing a design that is simultaneously large-scale and spacious, and one he exploited for the highly singular façade composition. The structural scaffold is combined here skillfully with a characteristic outer shell, at the same time making possible enormous spatial freedom within. Standing in the foreground here is not the academic declension of a construction, but instead its pragmatic appropriation and combination for the sake of achieving an extraordinary spatial and sculptural presence (p. 102).

EASY ADAPTABILITY

It is well known that the essential advantages of steel construction are its efficiency and adaptability, when structure, interior finishes, and technical installations are consistently separate. The Brick Leaf House impressively demonstrates these possibilities: the building contractor was able to prefabricate the steel structure and assemble it in just a few days with a pneumatic crane (p. 103). Subsequently, non-loadbearing infills and claddings were added to shape the individual rooms. During the entire building period, bathrooms, kitchen, and lighting were continuously adapted and optimized through discussions with the client. Even after completion, the installations in the ceiling cavity are permanently accessible, and can be adapted further. In contrast to solid construction, where all recesses and inserts must be defined and coordinated already for the shell construction, the steel structure of the Brick Leaf House remained open to modification up to completion—and even long afterwards. Twelve years after the move-in-date, the client exploited this advantage: the two units were joined to form a larger unit for a single family, and the western wing was radically reorganized in the process.

Niko Nikolla

Architecture: Jonathan Woolf Architects, Christopher Snow
Supporting structure: Price & Myers LLP

1 Kent Kleinman, Leslie Van Duzer (eds.): *Mies van der Rohe, The Krefeld Villas* (New York: Princeton Architectural Press, 2005).

2 Pamela Buxton, "Jonathan Woolf's Inspiration: Mies van der Rohe's Krefeld Villas, Germany," http://www.bdonline.co.uk/jonathan-woolf's-inspirationmies-van-der-rohes-krefeld-villas-germany/5027116.article (last accessed May 15, 2019).

3 Peter Meyer, "Zwei Stahlskelettbauten in Basel: Architekten Artaria und Schmidt, Basel," in: *Schweizerische Bauzeitung,* 24 (1929).

4 Benedikt Loderer, "Gelassene Grosszügigkeit, Vogesenschulhaus Basel-Stadt," in: *Hochparterre,* 7 (1994).

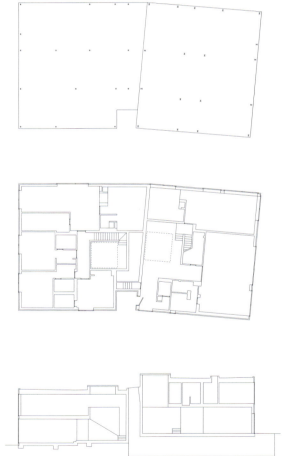
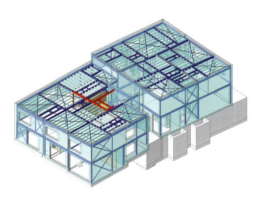

PRAGMATIC STRUCTURE

The steel structure prescribes no specific arrangement, but is instead adaptable to the architect's design. The consequence of this is an unsettled structural grid that is only comprehensible in the third dimension. Individual supports in the floors do not lay one on top of the next; open and closed profiles are used, and the arrangement of the ceiling panels appears arbitrary. While other projects in this book exemplify a stringent and didactic approach to steel construction, the Brick Leaf House demonstrates just how flexibly steel can be employed. Thanks to today's computer programs and production systems, a great variety of the different construction elements can be produced economically in small quantities, while the multiplication of individual units reduces costs only to a minimal extent.

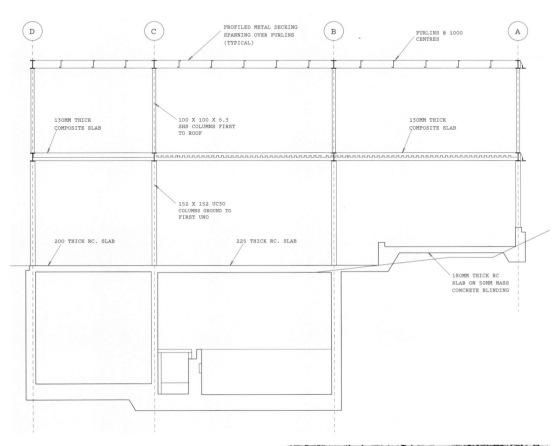

BUILDING PROCESS

The Brick Leaf House was erected according to a building method that is common in England: a solid, economical steel frame is produced by the contractor in the factory and then assembled on site in just a few days with a pneumatic crane. Superfluous here is heavy machinery of the kind that could potentially damage the garden or its imposing trees. Alterations during the construction process can be undertaken simply, since individual work categories are clearly separated from one another.

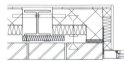
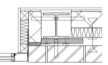

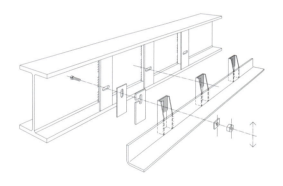

FAÇADE CONSTRUCTION

The material expression recalls typical Anglo-Saxon houses, with their white windows and dark brickwork. The double-shell construction fulfills the requirements of construction physics quite well, whereas the outer shell, consisting of painstakingly joined bricks, has no loadbearing or stiffening function. The formation of lintels and downstand beam becomes unnecessary, since the sections of the wall are carried by a concealed, circumferential steel bracket. This results in a linear thermal bridge, which is nonetheless unproblematic in terms of building physics since most of the girders are found in warm zones. The façade construction can be deciphered with reference to the circumferential expansion joints.

BRICK LEAF HOUSE   JONATHAN WOOLF ARCHITECTS

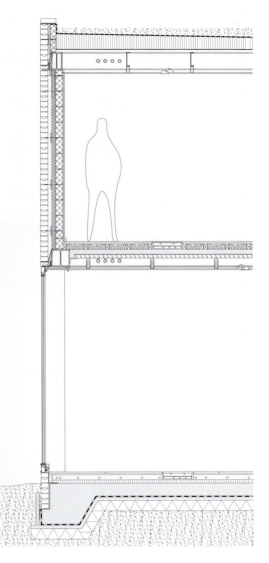

HYBRID CONSTRUCTION

The house's supporting structure consists of a slender, flexible steel frame. Like the external shell of the façade, the remaining materials on the interior are added without serving loadbearing or stiffening functions. The consistent separation between structure and space formation has advantages both with regard to the construction and to the building process: building-services installations can be simply installed in the streamlined ceiling system, and remain accessible for later adjustments. The lightweight walls and the cladding can be adapted or altered as needed. Last but not least, dry construction offers ecological benefits: weight is reduced, and recyclability ensured.

5

HOUSE WITH
THIN WALLS   MARTIN BÜHLER   106

5 Welded Walls

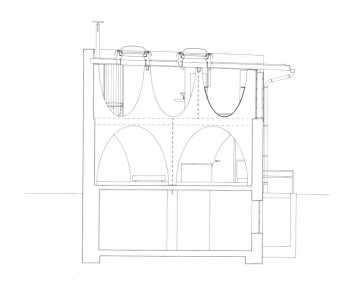

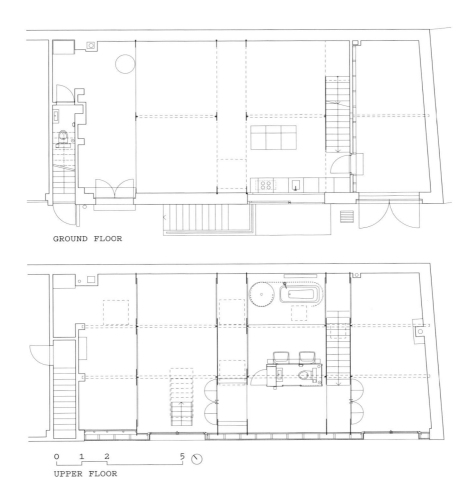

GROUND FLOOR

UPPER FLOOR

THE PLANAR USE OF STEEL

"Who would assert that the use of iron for beams and supports would be most advantageous in the form of rods?" asked Gottfried Semper in 1849, expressing skepticism concerning the suitability of iron for rooms with a "comfortable seclusion." He continues: "In the fine arts, this metal—aside from the aforementioned case of lightweight and delicate latticework—is usable only in the form of sheeting."[1] The modern mentality and its tectonics would seem to have refuted these ideas. Construction in steel is unavoidably associated today with girders, supports, and trusses. As a rule, the formation of space is detached from the primary construction, which is motivated not least of all by concerns about comfort levels in a steel building. All the more astonishing, then, that for his transformation of a commercial house with courtyard into a residence, Martin Bühler used expressively-shaped steel plates—which are almost as thin as sheet metal—as loadbearing internal walls. The design thereby unifies the supporting structure and the space formation in an idiosyncratic manner.

STRUCTURE AND CONTINUUM

The initial situation for the conversion suggested a minimization of construction area: five thin steel walls subdivide the house into functional zones and generate the maximum living space within a small area. The living areas are below, sleeping space above. Through the incision of two-story spaces and openings in the roof, light is admitted from above. Brightness pervades the interior volume, which opens up toward the sky rather than only toward the sides. The structural openings in the steel plates link the compartments to form a continuum. The experience of togetherness is consistently superimposed with a moment of privacy. Resulting via the sequence of living spaces and light wells is an astonishing sense of spatial depth, while the floor area is only 60 square meters (p. 109).

OLD AND NEW MATERIALITY

Martin Bühler's house is a conversion, not a new structure, and in a sense this circumstance is fundamental for its spatial quality. The physical presence of the pre-existing building provides a robust shell for the new structure. The history of this commercial building is accumulated in its materiality, and the physically arduous workmanship of the welded steel plates, welded on-site, is a response to this (p. 115).

In his house, Martin Bühler goes in search of sensual experience and beauty.[2] In the spirit of Henry van de Velde, the latter emerges through the "animation of the material": "Wood, metal, stone, and precious stones owe their singular beauty to the life that is infused in them through their processing, through the traces of tool marks, the various ways in which they express the enthused passion or sensibility of those who handle them."[3] And the awakening of this materiality emerges not least of all through an interplay with the light and rhythm of the space: "It occurs through the interplay of light and shadow, through the ratio of pale to dark surfaces, through gradations of values, which interrupt one another successively, and which determine the rhythm through the emphasis on individual moments […]."[4] All this is readily observable here.

The extreme thinness of the white steel plates and the precision and sharp-edged quality of the elliptical openings points toward the second postulate proffered by van de Velde—the development of the material in the direction of dematerialization. Bühler writes: "Steel plates have […] no palpable mass, their attractiveness, hence, resides in their form." Only the sensual side of form, he says, is capable of making the space visible.[5] In fact, the incisions—which at least initially appear to be purely formal in character—achieve more than the dissolution of the wall: not unlike stalactites and stalagmites, the directional openings can be associated first with an introverted grotto, and secondly with their upward striving toward the idyllic roof terrace. They stand equally for a spatial intention as well as for material fitness, since the search for a continuous laser cut integrates questions of digital manufacture into the design process (p. 114).

Clearly, however, total dematerialization is not the theme of this house. To be sure, Bühler strives for an abstraction of the surfaces—all of the walls are white, whether stone or steel, and the floor on the ground level is metallic, whether concrete or sheet metal. Nonetheless, the eye is continuously drawn toward constructive details and toward the tactile qualities of the old walls and floors (p. 113). It is not least of all the simultaneity of pre-existing and new structures that determines the narrative quality of the space, and makes it feel so comfortable.

Tanja Reimer

Architecture: Martin Bühler Architekt,
Sebastian Kofink
Supporting structure: Dr. Lüchinger + Meyer
Bauingenieure

1 Gottfried Semper, "Eisenkonstruktionen" (1849), in: *Wissenschaft, Industrie und Kunst und andere Schriften über Architektur, Kunsthandwerk und Kunstunterricht,* ed. Hans M. Wingler (Mainz/Berlin: Kupferberg, 1966), pp. 22–24.
2 See Martin Bühler, "Dinge: Über die doppelte Natur des Raums," in: *Werk, Bauen und Wohnen,* 6 (2012), pp. 38–43.
3 Henry van de Velde, "Die Belebung des Stoffes als Prinzip der Schönheit" (1910), in: *Zum neuen Stil* (Munich: Piper, 1955), pp. 169–176, here p. 169.
4 Ibid., p. 170.
5 Bühler, "Dinge" (see n. 2), p. 40.

URBAN IDYLL

Since the existing building touches the boundaries of the parcel, building law permits no volumetric expansions. Moreover, the upper-level, with its minimal ceiling height, was not usable as living space, and the existing openings were oriented onto the courtyard to the northeast. The restrained façade renovation betrays nothing about the steel structure within. Through the elimination of commercial utilization and the planting of cherry and apple trees, the courtyard space now becomes an idyll in the urban context.

SENSUAL EXPERIENCE

Objects and materials in the house are designed for sensuous experience: the flowing space on the ground floor is subdivided by explicit thresholds. Serving as a step, a metallic box marks the transition to the living area. In the form of shimmering intarsia sent into the floor, rolled, unfinished sheet aluminum is set off from the concrete thresholds, which are given a coat of metallic paint. In the upper level, small clamping profiles occassionally hold the glazing—which serves as a safety barrier—only in some places in front of the steel plates. As we gaze through the spatial layers, reflections on the glass produce spatial puzzlement. The bridge from the bathroom into the bedroom resembles a half-pipe, and consists of a curving sheet of steel 6 millimeters in thickness. Passage across the threshold thereby becomes both physically and acoustically perceptible. The most intimate room in the house is found in the cellar: in the top-lit sleeping niche for guests, nothing is to be seen of the expressive steel walls.

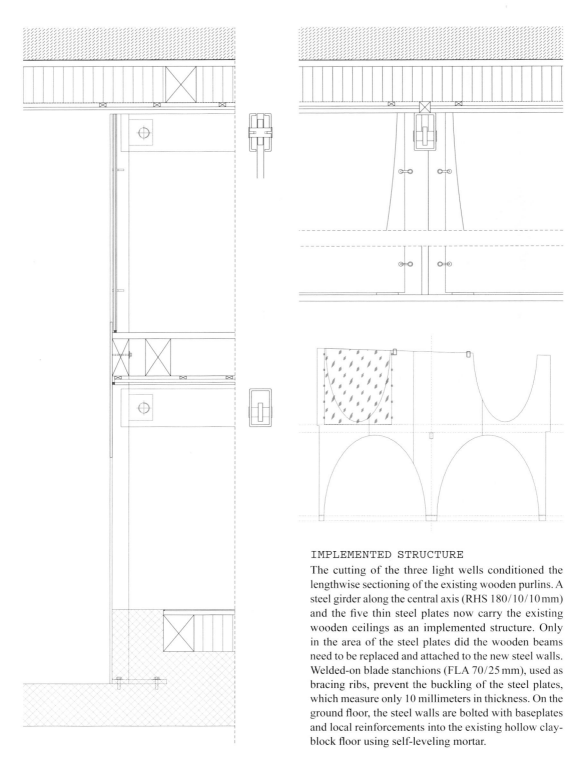

IMPLEMENTED STRUCTURE

The cutting of the three light wells conditioned the lengthwise sectioning of the existing wooden purlins. A steel girder along the central axis (RHS 180/10/10 mm) and the five thin steel plates now carry the existing wooden ceilings as an implemented structure. Only in the area of the steel plates did the wooden beams need to be replaced and attached to the new steel walls. Welded-on blade stanchions (FLA 70/25 mm), used as bracing ribs, prevent the buckling of the steel plates, which measure only 10 millimeters in thickness. On the ground floor, the steel walls are bolted with baseplates and local reinforcements into the existing hollow clay-block floor using self-leveling mortar.

CONSTRUCTION PROCESS

As interrelated elements, the steel walls were drawn and cut in the factory with a laser. Then the elements were split into assemblable and transportable pieces that could be welded together again at the building site. A number of workers and a cable pull were required to install the heavy elements, which weigh 200 to 400 kilograms. After a building period of six months, the house was ready for occupation.

6

RUA DO TEATRO   SOUTO DE MOURA   116

6   Paraphrasing a Building Tradition

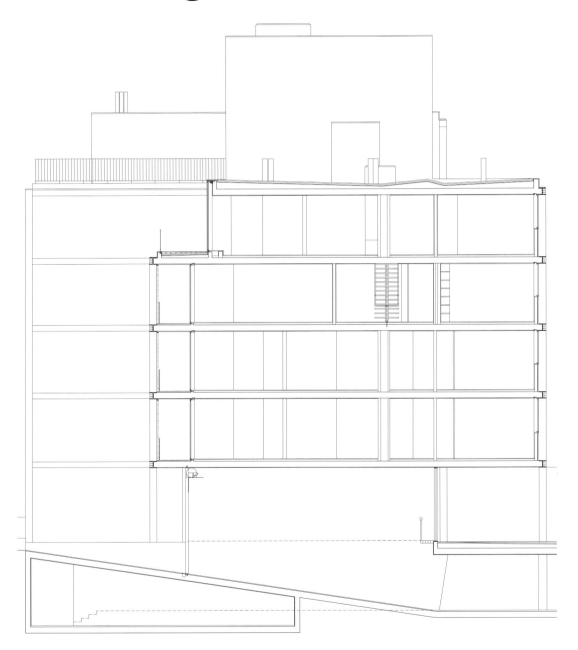

RUA DO TEATRO   SOUTO DE MOURA   118

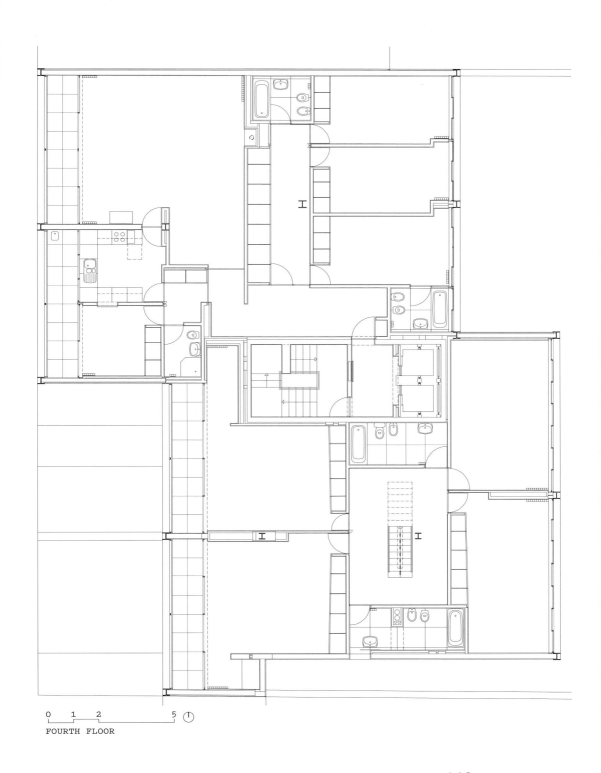

STEEL IN THE STONE CITY

Up to the present, it remains an architectural challenge to do justice with a steel construction to the conventions of a "stone city." For the architects of the Solothurn School of the postwar era, with their systematic design approach, it proved impossible: "They can't even imagine erecting a historicizing or 'adapted' building in Bern's old town,"[1] writes Ulrike Jehle-Schulte Strathaus about the Solothurn School. The view prevails that the structural characteristics of steel necessitates a solitary situation. A look at architectural history seems to confirm this view for the most part. The virtuoso steel buildings of Mies van der Rohe are exemplary in this regard.

Eduardo Souto de Moura is a self-professed admirer of Mies van der Rohe.[2] At the same time, this student of Álvaro Siza has been referred to repeatedly as an advocate of "Critical Regionalism"[3] —a term used by Kenneth Frampton to provide the field of tension between modernism and local tradition with a theoretical profile: "Critical Regionalism, […] while it is critical of modernization, nonetheless still refuses to abandon the emancipatory and progressive aspects of the modern architectural legacy."[4] Steel as a construction material is among the achievements of modern building. In Portugal, in particular, it was the Carnation Revolution,[5] resulting also from massive housing shortages, which gave rise to an interest in steel as an efficient building material. But how can this material engage in dialogue with a regional building tradition? Which resources can allow steel to find its role in a "stone city"?

The multifamily house on Rua do Teatro in Porto is a result of a skillful interpretation of local building traditions on the basis of a precise urban analysis. Already in his early years, Aldo Rossi's teachings opened up the city to Souto de Moura: "For me, to be a Rossian means to understand culture, the history of the city in which one lives, the place, memory, and to link all of these things together, and moreover according to a personal, emotional logic."[6] The Foz do Douro district is one of the areas that grew beyond the town limits of Porto already in the 18th century, due to pronounced urbanization processes. The typical development form consisted of narrow, deep parcels, which—through an alignment that runs crosswise to the topography—constituted a morphological response to local conditions.

NEW MATERIAL, OLD TRADITION

In order to inscribe the building into the small-scale structures of the vicinity, the main volumes are refined by the use of an offset, both in plan and vertically. A centrally configured support subdivides the frontward and setback façades again, so that their dimensions make reference to the locally typical front façades (p. 117). The traditional house front consists of pretreated granite blocks, which frame an either plastered of tile-clad façade surface with a base and corner pilasters. Also granite are the window openings, their jambs immovably anchored in these surfaces. The sizes of the openings are dependent upon the dimensioning of the lintels (p. 122). Souto de Moura characterizes the principles of his translation into steel construction as follows: "The building follows that same tradition, not as imitation, but as a constructive principle. The stone structure is replaced by steel […]."[7] The wide spans of the openings are determined now by the steel (p. 123). The setback section of the façade in the balcony area exposes the structure toward the street. Liberated in this way, it gives expression to its structural performance as a representative gesture, doing justice to the demands of a main façade. With steel, in contradistinction to a mural manner of construction, where the sculptural additions constitutes the ornamentation, this role is played by subtraction, by emptiness.

"[…] but the coating remains the same: zinc and slate."[8] The striking roof structures, clad in zinc sheet, play a central role when it comes to making the building compatible with the neighborhood, since their informal character counters the partially geometric quality of the steel structure (p. 124). Through this gesture, the building appropriates the language of an unpretentious architecture that is encountered primarily in urban interior courtyards. In keeping with this tradition, the exterior sidewalls as well are clad in slate shingle (p. 117). The building hence acknowledges urban conventions. This building material, meanwhile, can be ascribed an ambivalent impact: it gives the structure clear boundaries, at the same time opening up a dialogue with the urban fabric through a material reference.

On various architectonic levels, Souto de Moura interprets the traditional building style in the spirit of Critical Regionalism: "While opposed to the sentimental simulation of local vernacular, Critical Regionalism will, on occasion, insert reinterpreted vernacular elements as disjunctive episodes within the whole."[9] The steel skeleton becomes the organizing resource of this particular episode. Decisive for a successful outcome, however, is the constructive translation through which steel assimilates a traditional construction principle in a substantive way. But central as well is the taming of the structural performance capacity of steel. Only in this way can the constructive expression approximate to the surrounding urban scale. This process is fine-tuned through enrichment with local materials, so that the steel structure enters into an intriguing form of coexistence with the "stone city," thereby doing justice to one of Souto de Moura's architectural demands: "My wish is for a building to remain anonymous, which is the opposite of its remaining unnoticed."[10]

Patric Furrer

Architecture: Eduardo Souto de Moura, Graça Correia, Silvia Alves, Pedro Mendes, Francisco Cunha, Manuela Lara
Supporting structure: Codio

1   Ulrike Jehle-Schulte Strathaus, "Die Solothurner Schule," in: *Werk, Bauen und Wohnen,* 7/8 (1981), p. 11.
2   "I wanted to see everything by Mies van der Rohe, from the first of the last building." Interview with Souto de Moura for the exhibition *Souto de Moura 1980–2015* at the Raketenstation Hombroich, https://vimeo.com/125330614 (last accessed May 15, 2019).
3   See Akos Moravanszky, *Lehrgerüste: Theorie und Stofflichkeit der Architektur* (Zurich: gta, 2015), p. 350.
4   Kenneth Frampton, "Critical Regionalism: Modern Architecture and Cultural Identity," in same author, *Modern Architecture: A Critical History* (New York: Thames and Hudson, 1985), p. 327.
5   The Carnation Revolution was a response to grievances against the 40-year-long dictatorship of António de Oliveira Salazar. The widespread housing shortage was one of the motivations that drove people into the streets in 1974, ultimately causing the dictatorship to collapse.
6   Moravanszky, *Lehrgerüste* (see n. 3), p. 348.
7   Cited from the project description, written by Souto de Moura; translated from Portuguese by Francisco Ferreira.
8   Ibid.
9   Frampton, *Modern Architecture* (see n. 4), p. 372.
10 Werner Blaser, *Eduardo Souto de Moura: Stein Element Stone* (Basel: Birkhäuser, 2003), p. 26.

TRADITIONAL FAÇADES AS REFERENCE
The locally typical townhouse façades of Matosinhos[11] display a "typology of the wall as structure and as partition,"[12] which inspired Souto de Moura in his design for an apartment building on the Rua do Teatro.

HENCE STEEL
"After the revolution, […] when I became involved in discussions about the need to construct a half-million houses, it became clear that we would need a system, one that would be production-oriented, modular, and rational."[13] Accordingly, the building on the Rua do Teatro was conceived through and through as a steel structure. Cost pressures from the general contractor, however, impelled the builder to realize the ceilings in in-situ concrete. Nonetheless, it proved possible to assemble the steel structure in just three days. For this project, Souto de Moura also considered prefabrication with concrete.[14] This approach is, however, largely unknown in Portugal.

EMBELLISHED SKELETON

The steel structure becomes the means of organizing the building. Played through in a number of variations, it responds in a differentiated way to the immediate context. The rigid skeleton develops richly-faceted façades that oscillate between severity and nonchalance. On the street side, the structure renounces infills; the naked geometry of the structure is scenarized. The masonry lateral façades, with their white plaster surfaces, reference the masonry-and-partition-wall typology[15] of the traditional townhouse façades. The carrying capacity of steel is thereby made clear. Revived on the rear façades are images of traditional courtyard façades, with wooden balcony railings positioned upfront. Souto de Moura executes the railings in a vertically folded zinc sheet. Only on the outer sidewalls is the circumferential skeleton interrupted. Clad with locally typical slate shingles, it remains invisible.

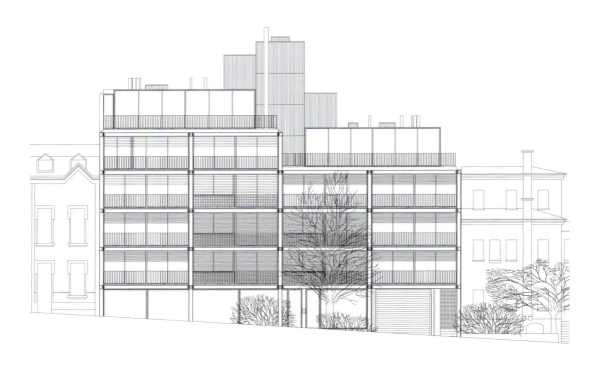

STEEL JOINS

Concerning architectonic joins, Ákos Moravánszky writes: "Emerging from the primary necessity of joining is the first technical object; the join resolves a task with the spatial calligraphy of the joins as a process that results in an ornamental form."[16] In the building on the Rua do Teatro, the joins come close to such technically-conditioned ornamental forms. The joins are visually accentuated through the additional stiffening plates. The plates extend the legibility beyond the banal joining of individual parts to the level of an interweaving of elements. Graça Correia, who served as project director at the time,[17] reports that the originally unplanned reinforcements were prescribed by a second engineer who reviewed the structural plans. Following intuitive investigations using a 1:1 model, Souto de Moura justified their existence with the argument that the building was intended as a technical formation, and that this should be allowed to come to expression.

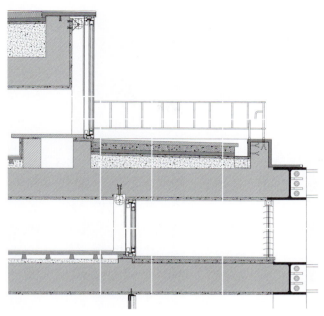

INTIMATIONS

The external presence of the steel awakens expectations within. With the exception of the visible supports, it is primarily the layout that profits from the freedom granted by the steel. As a direct carrier of atmosphere, it is barely developed, whereas subtle measures in the interior design allude to it repeatedly. All doors and built-in cabinets, for example, are room-height. This results in an acoustic weakening of the doors, due to the fact that the spatial intention precludes the use of door frames. Joins at the transition between wall and ceiling clarify the non-loadbearing status of the brick walls. Both measures can be understood as a correlation with the horizontal HEA-façade profiles, which are translated with precision on the inside with the concrete ceiling.

11 City north of Porto, which was organized rapidly in the late 19th century through the construction of the Port of Leixões.
12 See Blaser, *Eduardo Souto de Moura* (see n. 10), p. 8.
13 Souto de Moura, interview (see n. 2).
14 Souto de Moura's interest in prefabrication in concrete was awakened in Greece. At the request of Fernando Távora, who wanted to study the temple buildings once more before his death, Távora, Siza, and Souto de Moura undertook an educational trip to Greece.
15 See Blaser, *Eduardo Souto de Moura* (see n. 10), p. 8.
16 Ákos Moravánszky, *Graber Pulver: Werkstücke,* vol. 9 in the series "De aedibus" (Lucerne: Quart Verlag, 2005), p. 8.
17 Telephone conversation on November 25, 2015 with Graça Correia, PhD UPC-lecturer at the FAUP, Porto, and researcher at the LABART, ULP, Porto.

7

TERRACE HOUSE   ATELIER BOW-WOW

7 Framing and Filling

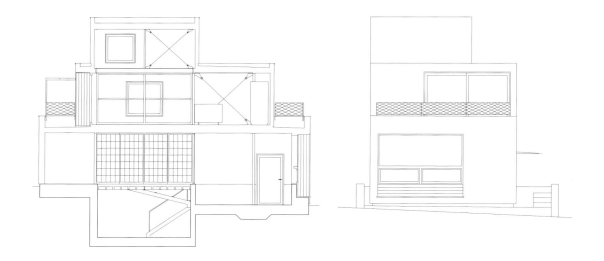

TERRACE HOUSE   ATELIER BOW-WOW

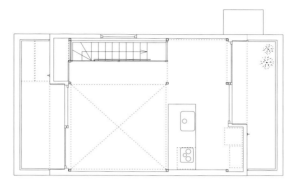

UPPER FLOOR

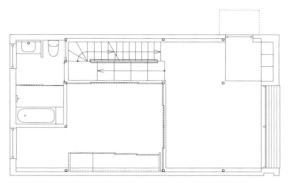

GROUND FLOOR

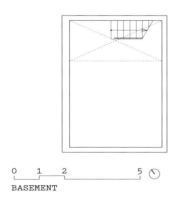

BASEMENT

LIVING TRADITION

The Terrace House by Atelier Bow-Wow stands in a residential district of Yokohama City that was formerly characterized by concrete terrace houses dating from the 1960s. The real-estate boom of recent decades, and the housing production that accompanied it, have transformed the morphology of the locale: today, the anonymous neighborhood is shaped by fenced-in, standardized single-family homes that appear unrelated to the street zone (p. 132). As a critique of this development, Momoyo Kaijima and Yoshiharu Tsukamoto conceived the Terrace House in reliance on the formerly prevalent type, and translated the staggered arrangement of the mural terrace house into a stack of three white plastered cubes.[1] At the client's request, it is based not on solid but instead on skeleton construction, and clad with rear-ventilated plaster-based paneling. Opening up within in a relationship of tension with the outside is the atmospheric warmth of the traditional Japanese house. The performance capacity of the steel allows the dimensions of the structural skeleton to be reduced to a minimum, emphasizing the surfaces between them all the more. The infill elements, consisting of Japanese linden wood and *shojis* spanned with rice paper, shape the spatial arrangement within (pp. 126-127). The hybrid steel-and-wood construction represents a transformation of a traditional building method and of the lifestyle that is bound up with it. The result is a unity of two contrasting materials, with the warmth of the wooden surfaces and the lightness and precision of the steel complementing one another symbiotically.[2] In a declaration of love for Japanese culture composed in 1933, Bruno Taut admired the capacity of the phenomena of life there to join together into a harmonious whole within a "living tradition."[3] The Terrace House seems to confirm this today as well.

ONE-ROOM HOUSE

In accordance with the traditional Japanese home, its conception as a one-room house avoids contained rooms. Together with the steel girders, fragile steel supports form a delicate scaffold, which, beginning from the freestanding supports in the entrance area, extend in all directions (p. 133). The structure defines the spaces of the house—in contradistinction to a regular axis system—with various precisely determined proportions (p. 129). The stairs, consisting of thin steel plates, are integrated nearly seamlessly into this structure. The result is a continuity which allows the space to seem larger than it is. The ground floor is subdivided by a disjunction in levels, resulting in a threshold between the studio and the sleeping area that creates privacy (p. 133). In the upper story, the living/dining room extends across the entire length from terrace to terrace, forming a center in the two-story area above the sleeping and storage room. Through the concrete base and the skylight, there is an intensive relationship to both floor and sky, thereby taking advantage of the available space in the vertical dimension (p. 135).[4]

ESTABLISHING RELATIONSHIPS

"Tsukamoto and Kaijima design exteriors as calculated responses to surrounding conditions. Their interiors are based on compositions of mediatory devices, not on the disposition of primary spaces. In short, their work is not an architecture of spaces, but an architecture of relationships."[5] With their deep embrasures, the façades establish a distance between inner and outer worlds. Occasionally, however, this distance is reduced: the building is opened up via large windows on the long axis. Views onto the street and across the terraces position the building and its inhabitants in relationship to the surroundings. The placement of the studio on the street façade makes possible—not unlike the *machiya*[6]—a combination of work and dwelling in the house, as well as a dialogue with the street zone (p. 133). Four subordinate square opaque windows in the side walls are situated within the field of the steel construction, bringing additional soft light into the interior. The distinction between light and view windows is a response to the close proximity of the adjacent homes (p. 135). Terraces displace a portion of private life into the outdoor space, and a bench in the window of the ground floor encourages conversations with neighbors. At twilight, warm light streams through the large openings from the interior onto the street. The apparent bonds betray the steel construction beneath the abstracted surface (p. 132).

Tanja Reimer

Architecture: Atelier Bow-Wow
Supporting structure: Matou Structural Engineers

1   By developing their "mini-house" projects in a fundamental sense from the context and the personalities of the clients, Kaijima and Tsukamoto enact a dialogue between the building and the city, as well as between the architecture and society. This attitude is evident in their research: "[…] the buildings that Atelier Bow-Wow deal with can be understood as media inscribed by their surrounding environments, by their sense of place, and by underlying political and economical dynamics. […] Cultivating the gaze of readers in this manner is […] linked to cultivating their literacy regarding macroscopic problems that underlie existing buildings and the city." Yoshikazu Nango, "Understanding Architecture as Medium," in: Atelier Bow-Wow, *The Architectures of Atelier Bow-Wow: Behaviorology* (New York: Rizzoli, 2010), pp. 326–328.

2   Via the atmospheric qualities of this material combination, composite construction in wood and steel open up constructive potential for an economical and ecological approach to building in the European context as well. See SZS Stahlbau Zentrum Schweiz (ed.), "Stahl und Holz: die neue Leichtigkeit," in: *Steeldoc,* 3/4 (2012).

3   See Bruno Taut, "Shinto: Reichtum in Einfachheit," in: *Ich liebe die japanische Kultur,* 2nd. ed. (Berlin: Gebr. Mann, 2004) pp. 77–91, here p. 77.

4   Bearing in mind our insulation regulations, the minimal insulation in the four slabs and roof seems astonishing. It almost appears as though the relationship to the floor and the sky was intensified in this way.

5   "The Origins of Atelier Bow-Wow's Gaze," in: Atelier Bow-Wow, *The Architectures of Atelier Bow-Wow* (see n. 1), p. 128.

6   The *machiya* is a traditional Japanese townhouse type with integrated work room or shop. See Meruro Washida, "Machiya," in: Laurent Stalder, Cornelia Escher, Megumi Komura, Meruro Washida (eds.), *Atelier Bow-Wow: A Primer* (Cologne: Walter König, 2013), pp. 108–110.

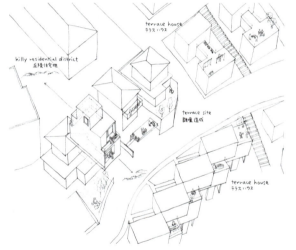

FOREVER NEW

In Japanese culture, the cycle of life is valued somewhat differently than in Europe. In the ecological context, the reuse of materials is more relevant than claims to permanence. While the Metabolism movement of the 1960s and 1970s relied upon the flexibility of built structures, in evidence today is instead a void metabolism,[7] with small-scale parcel structures forming the basis for a generational approach to building. In their projects, Atelier Bow-Wow searches for the societal as well as special potential of this smallness,[8] implementing it in their mini-houses.[9] Here lies the opportunity for anchoring building in the lifestyle of human beings, and at the same time for the radicalization of architectural concepts. Steel appears to be a suitable building material in this context.

SURFACE AND STRUCTURE

The profiles, which have been given a white fire-protective coating and are visible as a combination of flanges and supports, form an abstract frame for the infill elements in wood. Guide rails for the *shojis* are integrated elegantly into the steel beams, while the floor surface, consisting of oak parquet, is almost flush with the structure. The building envelope is emphasized by stiffening braces which run behind the supporting structure, and are connected with it only on the ground floor at the interface with the town.

A SPATIALLY EFFECTIVE BASE

Inside, a concrete base mediates the disjunction of elevations as a kind of trough, raising the actual living spaces up from the floor. As in traditional houses, the structural elements of the skeleton construction are protected from the effects of moisture by a spatially effective base.

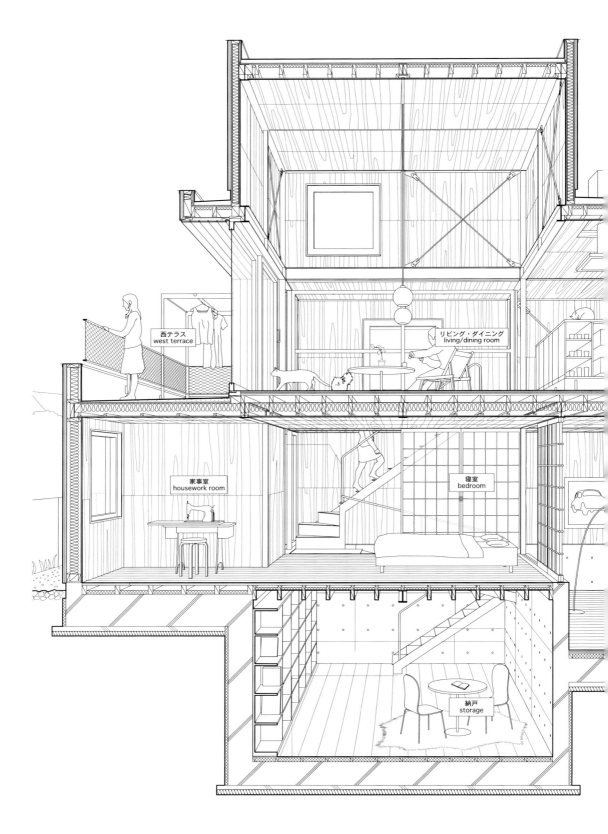

TERRACE HOUSE   ATELIER BOW-WOW   134

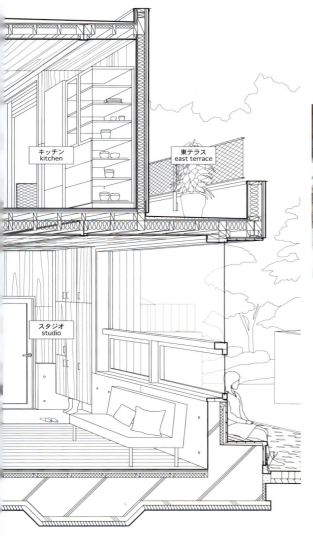

STANDARD PROFILES SPECIFICALLY JOINED

In the realm of construction with wood, Japan has an extensive culture of joining principles of which steel building can take advantage. Atelier Bow-Wow connect the supports in a direct fashion with cross-section profiles measuring 8 centimeters in width, and girders with a welded cross-piece and bolt. The construction is executed in an economical way, using standardized products but joining them in an individual fashion to form a painstakingly composed whole.

7   Yoshiharu Tsukamoto, "Void Metabolism," in: *Architectural Design,* 82 (2012), pp. 88–93.
8   Megumi Komura, "Smallness," in: Stalder et al., *Atelier Bow-Wow* (see n. 6), pp. 22–24.
9   "I treated smallness as a material (albeit one that differs from wood, concrete, or steel). While we can work with materials, we cannot create them as we please. We should strive to understand them and gain a firm grasp of their properties." Yoshiharu Tsukamoto, *chiisana ie no kizuiki* (Tokyo: Ōkokusha, 2003), here pp. 79–80.

8

APARTMENT BUILDING — GRASER ARCHITEKTEN

8   Dressed in Metal

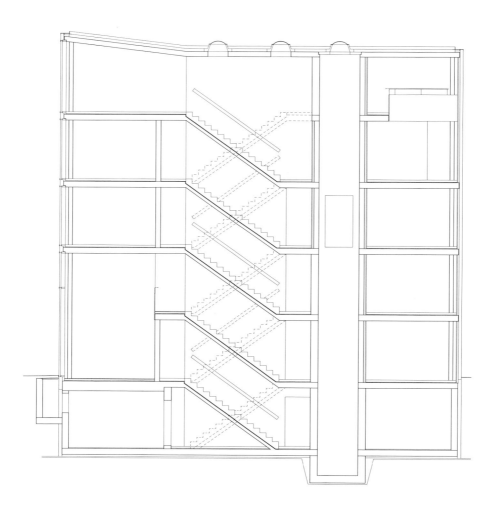

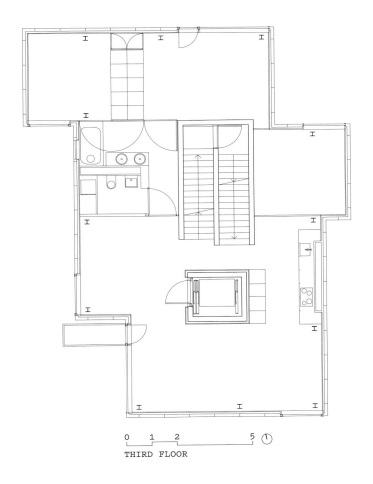

THIRD FLOOR

SYSTEMIC REVITALIZATION

With its remarkable appearance, Jürg Graser's multifamily dwelling is an astonishing sight in this urban residential district. It seems to be from a different era: the thin outer walls suggest the absence of any standards regarding thermal insulation. The porthole windows and rounded corners recall the machine aesthetic of modernism, and the metallic quality of its façade the buildings of Jean Prouvé. Nor do its railings or awnings seem to belong to our own time (pp. 136-137). Undeterred by current trends, Jürg Graser strives to achieve a characteristic architecture through structural logic, formal reduction, and technical precision. Even early on, he was fascinated by the Solothurn School and its protagonists. Recently, with his publication *Gefüllte Leere* (filled emptiness), he made a major contribution to the study of Swiss postwar architecture, calling attention again to the qualities of these buildings.[1] But while so-called "Jura southern-foothills architecture" was preoccupied in particular with continuous systematization on the basis of industrial modes of production, Graser regards spatial dramaturgy within consummate form to be of equally great significance.

MULTIPLICITY DESPITE STRINGENT ORGANIZATION

The building's outer form, however, offers few hints concerning its internal complexity. Three spacious double-story, so-called "maisonette" apartments interpenetrate volumetrically, and are supplemented on the ground floor by a studio apartment. Each maisonette enjoys a private outdoor space, and is multi-sided in orientation. Overlapping in a helix configuration within the massive access core are internal and public staircases, generating four contrasting entrance situations (p. 144). Despite the dense development of the parcel, this makes it possible to translate the qualities of the single-family home into a multistory, multiunit dwelling. At least initially, the complexity of the individual dwellings seems to contradict the serial character of the system construction, but it is precisely the balancing act between these two poles that accounts for the project's charm.

CONVERTING SYSTEMS

The use of industrial construction systems in residential building is a rarity. Through the Werkhalle in Regensdorf, Jürg Graser was already able to accumulate experience with standardized composite panels, and to familiarize himself with the advantages and drawbacks of this approach to building, which is suitable in particular for the economical enclosure of large volumes (p. 142).[2] But the pragmatic joining and assembly with sheet metal and covering strips which is familiar in the commercial context would have contradicted the perfectionism sought by the architects, as well as their demand for urbanistic integration into a residential district. Through an arrangement of diverse systems and building methods, Graser succeeded in exploiting the advantages of commercial products while compensating for their weaknesses.

The supporting structure is formed by a massive core in conjunction with the attached concrete ceilings and peripheral steel stanchions (p. 144). The stanchions replace the loadbearing outer wall, making possible the slim assembly of the curtain wall from industrial composite panels. On the inside, in order to reduce sound transfer, the panels are combined with a further system-based construction method involving gypsum plasterboard. Seen from within, the modular curtain wall hence becomes a seamless wall surface that conveys homogeneity and tranquility, but whose massive appearance behind the stanchions is also perplexing (p. 145).

For the façade design, Graser refines the industrial construction method, adapting to the new context (p. 143). This was

GRASER
APARTMENT BUILDING ARCHITEKTEN

possible only because the elaboration of constructive and design questions were synchronized from the very beginning. The vertical panels prescribed a stringent grid for the design of the floor plan. The renunciation of horizontal joins in the façade endows the volume with elegance, at the same time however limiting the building's height to 15 meters. While with commercial buildings, the connections to other parts of the building and corners serve as buffer zones for dimensional tolerances, and can be disguised with sheet metal, such room to maneuver is absent here. Only in the area of the vertical of the uninterrupted glass fronts can tolerances be accepted to a minimal degree. The corner solution involves a brilliant special design: a wedge is milled out in the middle of the panel, which is then bent 90 degrees along this edge. This creates the rounded corners which give the building its idiosyncratic machine aesthetic.

To equal degrees, the project demonstrates both the possibilities and challenges associated with the use of industrial systems for multistory apartment buildings. Thanks to this spirit of constructive invention and meticulous execution, the building succeeds in its context as a wayward character while offering a superior level of comfort within.

Niko Nikolla

Architecture: Graser Architekten, Jürg Graser, Beda Troxler
Supporting structure: Marti + Dietschweiler AG
Construction physics: Bau Energie Umwelttechnik Herrmann

1   Jürg Graser (ed.), *Gefüllte Leere: Das Bauen der Schule von Solothurn* (Zurich: gta, 2014).
2   Caspar Schärer, "Nischen der Gestaltung: Neubau Industriehalle in Regensdorf von Graser Architekten," in: *Werk, Bauen und Wohnen,* 7/8 (2010), pp. 62–64.

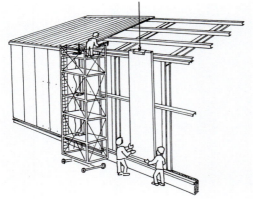

BUILDING SYSTEM

The composite panels employed consist of an inner and an outer sheet of metal with a layer of rigid foam insulation in between. Their minimal weight and superior rigidity allow large spans and simple assembly. This wall system finds broad application in industrial and commercial buildings, where short building schedules and economical budgets are called for. The elements are assembled by means of tongue-and-groove connections, and concealed bolts are used in the area of the butt joints.

ADAPTING THE SYSTEM

Graser does not make use of the catalog solutions of suppliers, but instead manipulates the panels in conformity with his architectonic vision, for example with the corner solution. For one of the window back fillets as well, the tongue-and-groove formations had to be adapted—they were trimmed or combined with an adapter profile. Conversely, it was possible to simply cut windows into the surfaces of the composite panels without compromising the joins or stability. The building's construction with its many projections and recesses results in a whole range of special solutions.

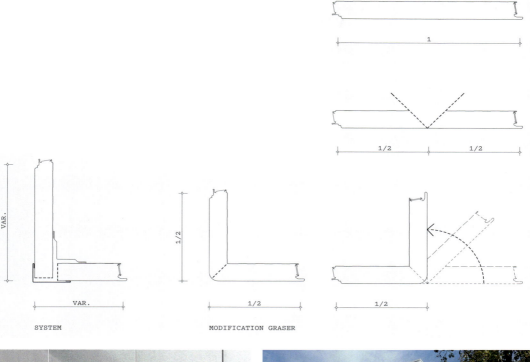

SYSTEM   MODIFICATION GRASER

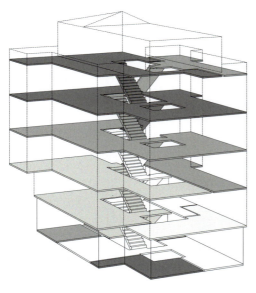

CONSTRUCTION AND BUILDING PROCESS

A stringent grid runs through the entire project, all the way to the formwork of the exposed concrete ceilings, and also determines the orientation of the open steel profile supports. Dimensional tolerances could not be absorbed by the joins of the panels, since these had to be compressed at the rabbet throughout the entire height of 15 meters in order to achieve the necessary tightness. Solid construction, in contrast, involves less precision of the kind that must be taken into account from the beginning. Serving as a buffer zone within the system are the vertical, continuous glass fronts, which escape the rigid grid.

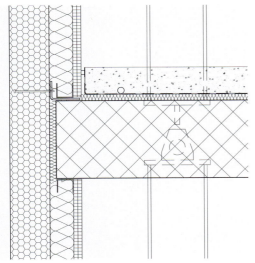

BUILDING PHYSICS REQUIREMENTS
The combination of various building systems and materials made it possible to satisfy current requirements concerning energy consumption, sound levels, and fire proofing. Only through the drywall construction could the lightweight panels achieve the minimum requirements for sound insulation. In order to prevent the vertical transmission of sound, the two systems were decoupled from one another. A subsequent noise measurement showed that the theoretical assumptions could be met at the critical points.

FIREPROOF COAT
In order to achieve the legally required fire resistance of R60, the loadbearing profile steel supports were given a fire-protection coating. This application, which forms an insulating layer, foams up in case of fire and requires an open space that must be specified. In response to the inconsistency of products and workmanship, fire-protection regulations were recently tightened in this regard. The Building Insurance of the Canton of Zurich has issued a directive concerning the application of fireproof coats as required for compliance with the legal constraints on property ownership inscribed in the land registry. Jürg Graser's multifamily dwelling was realized under the former fire-safety standards, without any entry in the land registry.

9

APPARTEMENT V3   MADE IN

9   Shimmering Character

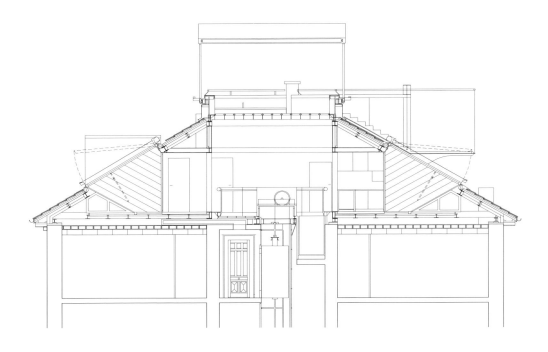

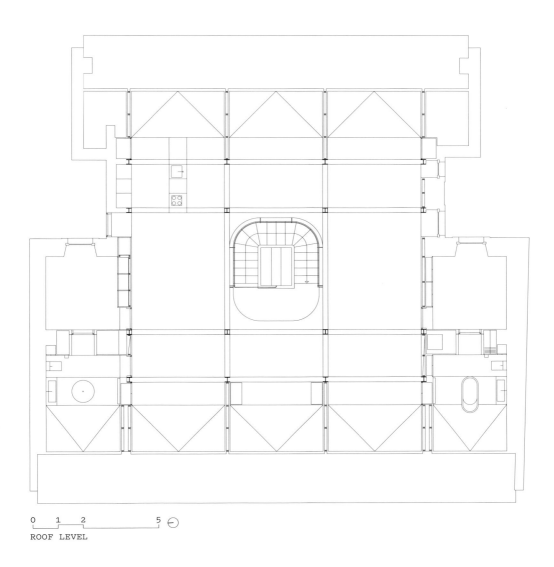
ROOF LEVEL

ABOVE THE ROOFS OF GENEVA

One of the greatest challenges of our times is the investigation of concepts for a high-quality densification of our cities. It is here that vertical additions to existing buildings can make a valuable contribution—something that has been shown repeatedly in the urban history of Geneva.[1] The Appartement V3 by Made in is exemplary of another phenomenon: during the real-estate boom of recent years, vertical additions have led to impressive profits in the upper price segment. In the process, the attic story has evolved into become the new *bel étage*. Although the building, which dates from 1914, had no reserves for expansion, and interventions had to respect the building line of the existing pitched roof, the project embodies the attitude, correspondingly, of a penthouse (p. 152). Following an initial restrained variant, it was decided to venture a *tabula rasa* up to the firewalls in order to create a new upscale apartment for a financially sound tenant.

MORE THAN STRUCTURE

Steel constructions possess technical advantages, which can be exploited for vertical additions: industrial prefabrication makes possible a short-term, low-emission, and dry construction site. Large span widths with minimal weight cope well with a precise load transfer to the existing walls, which in many instances obviates the need to reinforce the foundations. An efficient supporting structure can be realized in a restricted space and in a brief period of time. Often, these advantages can be achieved through wooden constructions as well—here, therefore the choice of steel as a material is not determined solely by practical considerations. The loadbearing structure also constitutes the atmospheric point of departure for the project. With reference to the Villa Chardonne, the architects have discussed their preference for "strong structures":[2] "Once the structure has arrived at a coherent expression in the form of the construction, the secondary elements can be derived from it. You could almost formulate it in extreme terms by saying that the Villa Chardonne is nothing but structure."[3] There, the Vierendeel trusses unified the supporting structure, the façade, and the spatial organization. With the vertical addition in Geneva, four girder beams subdivide the main space into three areas: a central area for arrival, another for cooking and eating, and a living room. The spacious staircase and the skylight turn entering into a dramaturgical act at the center of the apartment (pp. 146-147). Adjoining in the area of the firewalls are two small ship's-birth-style rooms, each measuring only 10 square meters, with luxurious bathrooms (p. 149).

Primary and secondary structures do in fact also form the spatial framework. Through the precise masking of individual elements, however, the archetype of the slanted attic space is overwritten geometrically—the supporting core form is not always congruent with the sought-after artistic form (p. 147). Emerging both constructively and spatially is a discrepancy between inner and outer silhouette:[4] the artistic form is defined—without reference to the context—from within and toward the outside, and is oriented exclusively toward the sky (p. 155).

The supporting structure is abstracted to become the element which characterizes the space, with pillars and trusses joining to form an angular grid. Behind the cladding, consisting of translucent metal mesh, the structure is joined with high-performance welded and visible bolted connections in a pragmatic and space-saving way (p. 153), while the space-determining supports are articulated in a sharp-edged way by sealing the HEB profiles with sheet metal. The undogmatic construction accentuates material characteristics, endowing the steel with a quality that is characteristic of this project.

In combination with the stone-like appearance of the artificial resin flooring and the mirrored surfaces of the skylight windows, the apartment makes a fascinating, sophisticated impression—one that is diametrically opposed to the rustic character of an attic (p. 154).

HUMAN AND MACHINE

Via a diving-board-style stair projecting from the roof, one reaches the spacious roof terrace, with its majestic view of the city, which functions as a counterweight to the introverted casket of the interior. Earlier, with the collage and slogan "Some don't work with the same gravity,"[5] Made in presented the Villa Chardonne as an object that remained unlocalizable—not unlike a spaceship—by virtue of its machine-style "prostheses."[6] Fictive elements (like the extendable bridge that serves as an entrance) are found in this project, as well in the form of the mirrored skylight windows, which are operated hydraulically, and the movable "wing-like" solar sail on the roof terrace (p. 155). Systems borrowed from mechanical engineering are manipulated and utilized for their specific symbolic value. "The machine is deployed as an artifice for the sake of a specific dramaturgy,"[7] one that breathes life into the project.

With this idiosyncratic dwelling, Made in seems to be in a sense projecting a portrait of the tenant, whose character oscillates between extravagance and social convention, translating this polarity in striking ways into spaces for retreat, and others for staging one's life. The dramaturgical architecture, however, culminated in a tragedy of sorts with the project's interruption: the client, presumably in search of a more reliable investment, withdrew shortly before completion.

Tanja Reimer

Architecture: Made in
Supporting structure: Moser Ing.
Metal construction: Stephan AG, AAV
Contractors, CMA SA
Façade engineering: Préface

1. On the urban history of Geneva with reference to vertical additions, see: Markus Moser et al., *Aufstocken mit Holz: Verdichten, Sanieren, Dämmen* (Basel: Birkhäuser, 2014), pp. 18–20.
2. Herzog & de Meuron have discussed the potential of steel for "strong structures" with reference to the "Bird's Nest" in Beijing—"Its appearance is pure structure." See Arthur Rüegg, "Starke Strukturen," in: *Werk, Bauen und Wohnen,* 5 (2009), pp. 4–11, here p. 6.
3. See Made in, interviewed in: Marc Angélil, Jörg Himmelreich, Departement für Architektur der ETH Zürich (eds.), *Architekturdialoge: Positionen – Konzepte – Visionen* (Sulgen: Niggli, 2011), pp. 206–221, here p. 221.
4. See Jaques Lucan, "Äussere und innere Silhouette. Anmerkungen zum Poché, zum Rosé im Schnitt," in: Barbara Burren, Martin Tschanz, Christa Vogt, ZHAW Zentrum Konstruktives Entwerfen (eds.), *Das schräge Dach: Ein Architekturhandbuch* (Sulgen: Niggli, 2008), pp. 136–143.
5. The architects conceived the collage and the slogan for the publication of the project in *Casabella.* See Made in, interview (see n. 3), p. 212.
6. See department lecture by François Charbonnet, among other topics on "prostheses" in their architecture, ETH Zurich, November 24, 2009, https://www.arch.ethz.ch/news-und-veranstaltungen/departementsvortraege/Bauten_bauen/ Made-in-Sarl.html (last accessed May 15, 2019).
7. Ibid.

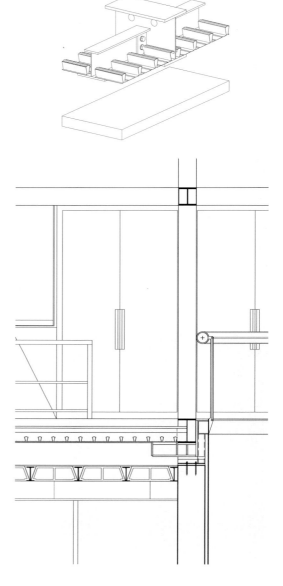

CONSTRAINT AND EFFICIENCY

Building regulations determine the external silhouette of the project, and its downtown location the conditions for its realization—the shell construction had to be completed quickly and efficiently. The legal building line was fully exploited, and the permissible degree of openness exhausted in order to bring light into the attic space. With its skylight windows, the new structure is detached from the rhythm of the façade, yet maintains the restraint appropriate to the roof area.

DISTRIBUTION LEVEL

To save space, the optimized floor structure could be integrated at the girder height of 20 centimeters through cast trapezoidal plates, where it reinforces the supporting structure as a distribution level. The rigidity of the construction improves the acoustics of the ceiling. The efficiency of the structure is particularly relevant, since the privatization of the attic story (as an apartment) requires an airspace underneath the new floor structure for the sake of smoke extraction in the existing staircase.

APPARTEMENT V3   MADE IN   152

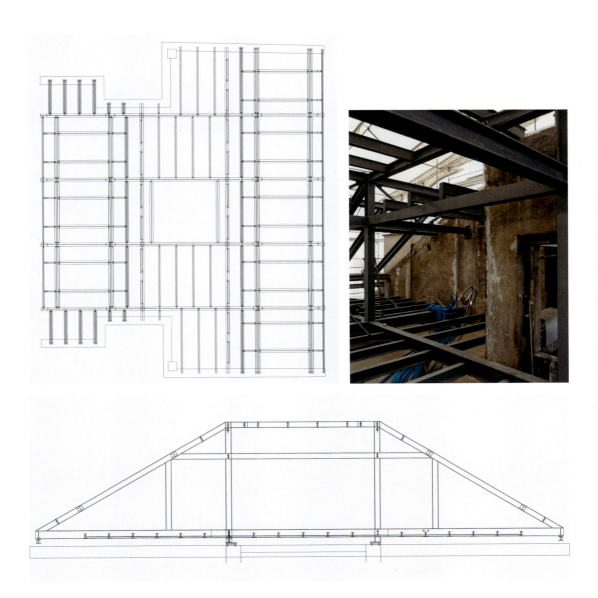

SUPPORTING STRUCTURE

The four prefabricated space trusses, each measuring approximately 17 meters and consisting of welded HEB profiles, span the attic space and lie on top of the staircase walls as well as being connected by a loadbearing truss to the external wall. The rhythm of supports, and hence the load transfer points, were taken over from the existing wooden structure. The main girders were bolted on site to the secondary structure, consisting of IPE profiles, which were embedded laterally into pocket supports in the firewalls. The shell structure was assembled solely with the help of a pneumatic crane.

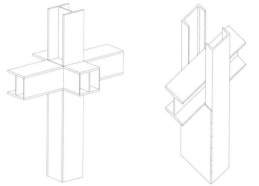

PRAGMATISM AND INTENSIFICATION

The bottom beams having the widest spans define the basic dimension of the spatial grid, whereby the supports with 20-centimeter edge lengths are slightly oversized. The abstraction of the visible grid is achieved by enclosing the HEB profiles with welded-on metal sheet followed by grinding. The result is a sharp-edged appearance, whose origins can be found in the representative-abstract tectonics of the supports in the Maison Clarté,[8] but which is quite removed from the theme of joining (see comparison on the left). At the same time, the mode of construction reflects the technical possibilities of our time, when welding vanishes from the building site, computer calculation optimizes the supporting structure pragmatically, and, at the same time, special solutions are once again becoming economically competitive. The planned finishing variant, involving circumferential mirrored panels on the central supports, would have driven the oscillation between a clattering *mis en scéne* and camouflage to extremes.

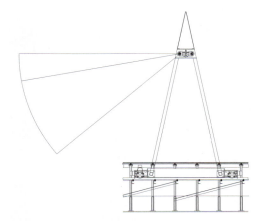

SKYLIGHT

Through the calculated deployment of daylight, the space reaches upward into the sky. A translucent, accessible skylight in specially developed glass with an anti-slip pattern, carried by filigree 8-millimeter steel bars, illuminates the space and sets it into relationship with the roof terrace above. The skylight windows reinforce the rhythm of the structure and, via the inclined mounting of the mirrored surfaces, admit light deep into the space.

SHADOW MACHINE

The volume of the former skylight lantern, made available by the relevant building regulations, was used to create an adjustable sunshade on the roof terrace, which can be used not least of all to ensure that the interior space does not become overheated by zenithal light entering from above. Above the substructure of the railing, the crane track is bolted directly to the supporting structure: the loads of the heavy structure, which weighs circa 1,800 kilograms, must the transferred. A sharp-edged U-profile forms the horizontal level of the balustrade, to which a steel tube is bolted like a guardrail. Clad flush with sheet metal and painted matte bluish-gray, the balustrade delimits a space that recalls a ship's deck.

8   Wolfgang Schett, Christian Sumi, Bruno Reichlin, "Architektur + Konstruktion," in: *Werk, Bauen und Wohnen*, 11–1992, p. 41–48.

EDITOR

Institute of Constructive Design / Institut Konstruktives Entwerfen (IKE)
The IKE sees itself as an interactive hub for design and constructive knowledge, and has been conducting research in this area since 1997. It is committed to an overarching occupational profile for architects and structural engineers with a focus on the "building culture of today". Close cooperation among architects, structural engineers, and thematically related experts anchored in practice and teaching provides the basis for a well-grounded engagement with constructive questions in research and teaching.

AUTHORS

Ingrid Burgdorf studied architecture at the ETH in Zurich. Since 1991 she has had her own architecture office in Zurich. She wrote a research paper on the Casa Il Girasole by Luigi Moretti, and received the Swiss Federal Prize for Fine Arts in 1998. She was a graduate assistant to Peter Märkli / Markus Peter at the ETH in Zurich for many years. Since 2007, she has been a lecturer in the Master's Program in Architecture at the ZHAW.

Patric Fischli-Boson studied structural engineering at the HSR in Rapperswil. Since 2015, he has directed the Swiss Center for Steel Construction in Zurich and Lausanne. Together with Christoph Büeler, he runs an engineering office in Schwyz. He presides over the SIA's structural engineers' professional group, and has been a lecturer in architecture at the ZHAW since 2016.

Patric Furrer studied architecture at the ZHAW, the UdK in Berlin, and the UPV in Valencia. He is a research associate at the IKE, and together with Andreas Jud runs the office Furrer Jud Architects in Zurich.

Marcel Meili (1953–2019) studied architecture at the ETH in Zurich. He ran an independent architecture office together with Markus Peter in Zurich since 1987, establishing a second office in Munich in 2006. Since 1999, he had been a professor in architecture at the ETH Zurich. He is the author of numerous essays and publications, and together with Markus Peter, he was awarded the Grand Prix Kunst / Prix Meret Oppenheim by the Swiss Federal Office of Culture in 2019 for their outstanding contribution to Swiss architecture.

Daniel Meyer studied structural engineering at the ETH Zurich and is the co-founder of Dr. Lüchinger + Meyer in Zurich. He is a lecturer at the ZHAW, a researcher, and serves on numerous committees.

Niko Nikolla studied architecture at the ZHAW in Winterthur. He was a research associate at the IKE until 2018 and runs his own architecture office in Winterthur.

Tanja Reimer studied architecture at the TU Darmstadt and the ETH in Zurich. She has been a research associate at IKE since 2015 and has headed the architectural firm Donet Schäfer Reimer Architects together with Pablo Donet and Tim Schäfer since 2018. In 2014, together with Lisa Euler she published *Klumpen. Auseinandersetzung mit einem Gebäudetyp,* in connection with a BSA research grant.

Astrid Staufer studied Architecture at the ETH in Zurich. Together with Thomas Hasler she has run the architectural firm Staufer & Hasler in Frauenfeld since 1994, and has held a double professorship with him at the TU Vienna since 2011. Since 2015, she has also headed the IKE at the ZHAW, since 2017 together with Andreas Sonderegger. From 2009 to 2016 she was president of the editorial committee of *Werk, Bauen + Wohnen.*

Martin Tschanz holds a PhD in architecture from ETH Zurich, worked as an assistant at the gta Institute and editor of architectural journals such as *Archithese* and *Werk, Bauen + Wohnen.* He lectures at the ZHAW on architectural theory, history, and criticism, and his work is published regularly in professional journals. In 2015, he published *Die Bauschule am Eidgenössischen Polytechnikum* Zürich.

PARTICIPANTS IN THE
SUMMER WORKSHOP:
RE-DOMESTICIZING STEEL

ZHAW

Tanja Reimer (project head), Patric Furrer, Jürg Graser, Marc Loeliger, Stephan Mäder, Daniel Meyer, Niko Nikolla, François Renaud, Alain Roserens, Astrid Staufer, Martin Tschanz, and Beat Waeber

PARTICIPANTS

Johan van Rompaey (University of Antwerp), Christian Frost (Birmingham City University), Alessandro Columbano (Birmingham City University), Pere Joan Ravetllat (ETSAB Barcelona), Cristina Pardal (ETSAB Barcelona), Francisco Ferreira (University of Minho), Carlos Maia (University of Minho) as well as thirty-one students from Antwerp, Barcelona, Birmingham, Guimarães, and Winterthur

EXPERT PANEL GUESTS

Martin Bühler (architect), Jürg Graser (Graser Architects), Jan De Vylder (De Vylder Vinck Taillieu), Frank Escher (Escher GuneWardena Architecture), Patric Fischli-Boson (Swiss Center for Steel Construction / SZS), Prof. Dr. Mario Fontana (ETH Zurich), Patrick Heiz (Made in), Megumi Komura (architect), Denis Kopitsis (Kopitsis Bauphysik), Marcel Meili (Meili & Peter Architects), Prof. Dr. Martin Mensinger (TU Munich), Prof. Dr. Joseph Schwartz (ETH Zurich, Dr. Schwartz Consulting), Chris Snow (Jonathan Woolf Architects)

ACKNOWLEDGMENTS

We would like to thank all of the participants in the summer workshops for their valuable contributions and ideas, as well as for their perspectives on the culture of steel construction coming from their respective countries. Frank Escher is owed particular thanks for his valuable support in the research on the Eames House, as well for his inspiring lecture on the Case Study Houses.

We are also most grateful to the contemporary architects of the case study projects for generously providing documents and information on their buildings. Our special thanks go to the clients, who allowed us to visit their buildings.

We'd also like to thank the authors of the icon texts for their valuable perspectives on these timelessly relevant buildings. They, in turn, are grateful to Patric Furrer, Niko Nikolla, and Tanja Reimer for supporting their research.

We thank Andreas Mühlebach, and Steffi Anton of Mühlebach Structural Engineering for their structural engineering advice during the analysis of the case studies, and Peter Frischknecht of PBK for assistance with questions of economy. Aurel Marti and François Renaud deserve our gratitude for their help with the French edition, and we thank Nicolas Baumann for his work on the plans done on short notice.

We thank the foundation of the former HSZ-T in Zurich, and the School of Architecture, Design and Civil Engineering of the ZHAW, specifically Stephan Mäder, for their generous support and funding for this project. Last but not least, we thank Stahlpromotion Schweiz, and the Stahlbau Zentrum Schweiz (SZS) for their financial support, and in particular Patric Fischli-Bosson for his inspiring and devoted collaboration.

IMAGE CREDITS

HÔTEL TASSEL
All works by Victor Horta © 2019, ProLitteris, Zurich
pp. 22–26, and 32 top left: © KIK-IRPA, Brussels,
Zurich Central Library (BZ 15).
p. 30 top, and p. 32 top right from: L'Emulation, 1895
p. 30 top: Horta Museum Archive, Brussels
p. 32 bottom: Gilbert De Keyser © 2019, ProLitteris,
Zurich

MAISON DE VERRE
Plans pp. 42, 46: Kenneth Frampton
All images: Michael Carapetian

EAMES HOUSE
pp. 48–49, 50, and p. 54 top left: Julius Shulman
© J. Paul Getty Trust. Getty Research Institute,
Los Angeles (2004.R.10)
pp. 51, 52: © 2019 Eames Office LLC
(eamesoffice.com), photographer Timothy
Street-Porter
p. 4, top right: © HB-08535-B, Hedrich-Blessing
Collection, Chicago History Museum
p. 56: Truscon Steel Company
p. 58 center left: © 2019 Eames Office LLC
(eamesoffice.com), photographer: Timothy
Street-Porter
p. 58 center right: © 2019 Eames Office, LLC
(eamesoffice.com),
plans drawn by ZHAW following original design

MÜLLER HOUSE
Plans: Christian Kerez
pp. 66–67, p. 74 top left and right, and p. 75 top and
center left: Georg Aerni
p. 72 top: Milan Rohrer
p. 72 bottom: Dr. Schwartz Consulting
p. 73: Schneider Stahlbau
p. 74: bottom right: Dr. Schwartz Consulting

53 HLM HOUSES LACATON & VASSAL
Plans: Lacaton & Vassal
pp. 76–77, p. 82 top, p. 84 top and center left, and
p. 85 top: Philippe Ruault
p. 83 center and bottom right: Lacaton & Vassal
p. 84 bottom left, and p. 85 bottom: Patric Furrer

SCHEEPLOS HOUSE
Plans: DVVT
All images: Filip Dujardin

BRICK LEAF HOUSE
Plans, and p. 103 bottom: Jonathan Woolf Architects
pp. 96–97, p. 104 bottom right, p. 105 top left, and
p. 105 bottom left: Hélène Binet

HOUSE WITH THIN WALLS
Plans und images: Martin Bühler
p. 112 left: Tanja Reimer

RUA DO TEATRO
Plans: Souto de Moura Office
pp. 116–117 and p. 123 top: Hisao Suzuki
p. 122 left: Werner Blaser
p. 122 top and bottom right: Graça Correia
p. 123 center right, p. 124 bottom right, p. 125 center
left: Patric Furrer
p. 123 center right: photographer unknown, from:
"Eduardo Souto de Moura: 1995–2005: la naturalidad
de las cosas," in El Croquis, no.124 (2005)

TERRACE HOUSE
Plans and images: © Atelier Bow-Wow

APARTMENT BUILDING
Plans: Graser Architekten
pp. 136–137, p. 143 bottom left and right, p. 145 top,
and p. 145 center right: Ralph Feiner
p. 142 top left, p. 142 right, p. 144 top, and p. 144
center right: Beda Troxler
p. 142 lower left: Montana Bausysteme AG

APPARTEMENT V3
Plans and images: Made in
p. 154 center left: ZHAW, based on documents
by Christian Sumi, Immeuble Clarté Geneva, 1932,
by Le Corbusier & Pierre Jeanneret, Zurich:
gta / Ammann, ETH Zurich, 1989
p. 155 bottom left: Walter Mair

In some cases, original plans have been slightly
graphically reworked by the IKE.
Despite best efforts, we have not been able to identify
the holders of copyright and printing rights for all
the illustrations. Copyright holders not mentioned
in the credits are asked to substantiate their claims,
and recompense will be made according to standard
practice.

IMPRINT

Concept: ZHAW, Institute of Constructive Design /
Institut Konstruktives Entwerfen
Project direction: Tanja Reimer
Collaborators: Niko Nikolla, and Patric Furrer
Editorial board: Ingrid Burgdorf, Jürg Graser, Daniel
Meyer, François Renaud, Astrid Staufer, and Martin
Tschanz
Graphic design: Büro 146. Maike Hamacher, Valentin
Hindermann, Madeleine Stahel, Zurich
Translation into English: Ian Pepper, David Haney
Copy editing: Sabine von Fischer
Proofreading: Thomas Skelton-Robinson
Lithography, printing, and binding: DZA Druckerei
zu Altenburg GmbH, Thuringia

© 2019 ZHAW, Institute of Constructive Design /
Institut Konstruktives Entwerfen, and Park Books,
Zurich
© for the texts, the authors
© for the images, see image credits, p. 159

Park Books
Niederdorfstrasse 54
8001 Zurich
Switzerland
www.park-books.com

Park Books is being supported by the Federal Office
of Culture with a general subsidy for the years
2016–2020.

All rights reserved; no part of this publication may be
reproduced, stored in a retrieval system or transmitted
in any form or by any means, electronic, mechanical,
photocopying, recording, or otherwise, without the
prior written consent of the publisher.

English edition: ISBN 978-3-03860-145-6
German edition: ISBN 978-3-03860-013-8
French edition: ISBN 978-3-03860-014-5